Justify My Love

JUSTIFY MY LOVE

Sex, Subversion, and Music Video

Ryann Donnelly

Published by Repeater Books
An imprint of Watkins Media Ltd

Unit 11Shepperton House
89-93 Shepperton Road
London
N1 3DF
United Kingdom

www.repeaterbooks.com
A Repeater Books paperback original 2019
1

Distributed in the United States by Random House, Inc., New
York.

Cover design: Johnny Bull
Typography and typesetting: Frederik Jehle
Typefaces: Meriden LT Std, Arial

ISBN: 9781912248414
Ebook ISBN: 9781912248421

Printed and bound in the United Kingdom by TJ International Ltd because of mom, Linda Donnelly x

CONTENTS

X

PART ONE

X.

I am invisible to myself because I do not have cable in the woods. I am the 1995 MTV Video Music Awards. I am Courtney Love's makeup compact flying over a balcony, interrupting Kurt Loder's interview with Madonna. I am Madonna's discontent, her pursed, prude lips. I am a prude. I am Loder's petrified congeniality when he shouts, "HI COURTNEY!" down the couple of stories from which Love has impressively (for both her strength and gall) launched her shit at the queen of pop. Madonna (naturally wired for provocation, but insincere): "Should we let her come up?" Loder (The purest yes man. Tone deaf to sarcasm): "Yeah!" Madonna (now sincere): "No, don't. Please." Loder to Love: "Come on up!" Love ascends.

Satin is in this year. Madonna wears it in the shape of a turquoise Gucci dress shirt, unbuttoned down the length of her sternum. Her black bra is visible over each perfect mound of breast. This is the image of a shirt torn open in anticipation of other forms of opening and entry, paused and prolonged. Her black cigarette pants are satin too — a soft barrier to the diamond-hard dancer's musculature underneath. Courtney wears a black satin skirt so short and twirly that it exposes the high curve of her ass. Her matching satin shirt has lacy princess sleeves, and big, pastel violet bows in front. Madonna corrupts the masculine, and brings sex into view. Courtney subverts the feminine through its exaggeration and constant juxtaposition with her unpredictable, violent, compact-throwing-at-the-queen-of-pop body. The two speak in competitive insults, which Courtney acknowledges after several rounds by kneeling on the ground. She could never win, because she is indeed the more insultable, if not genuinely worse person, so she dramatizes her inevitable loss with the silent question: "Is this what you want?" The two briefly discuss their shoes at Madonna's suggestion, then Madonna leaves. Love is the brash instigator, and stubborn survivor of their encounter, but Madge gets some fair jabs in before she walks off set like a quitter.

It would have been hard to say who won this competition of "most intimidating woman in music" had Love not proceeded to fall face-first off her chair as she recounted her early sexual history with Ted Nugent. The failure was too human. I am Madonna's splayed gem-tone satin, and Courtney's satin-covered ass. I am Courtney's thrash and Madonna's sobriety. For a brief moment in 1995, oil met fire. Captured in the same space was Madonna's control, and the destruction of Love.

X.

I have translated this encounter through the obsession I have with these women, as they were then, which has never been sated by passive admiration. As a teenager, I undertook the project of understanding my unbidden ardor by trying to do what they did. It lead to this.

The title of this book was initially chosen as an ode to the Madonna song and video of same name. Though the question of how love is justified, explained, expressed, or earned, came to re-frame my approach to this narrative. What started as a book on subversive performances of gender in music video — an exploration of their aesthetics, justifications for their value and power — now marries that research with the lived experiences — the obsessions, the true love, the secrets, the sex — that informed it. I am going to begin by weaving between the two because many of the authors, theories, and questions explored here have been with me for a long time. I have thought about how they operate within and outside of conventional performance contexts. They have been applicable to how I have performed and observed performances of gender, sex, sexuality in real life. The occasional collapse of time for the sake of pace is the main liberty I have knowingly taken with the verity of these memories. The second and third sections of this book are the outgrowth of the personal narrative that precedes them.

Courtney first. I was at the intersection of Sleater-Kinney Road and Pacific Ave., a passenger in my mom's car, when the new Hole single was introduced on the radio — Seattle's 107.7, The End. I would turn thirteen in ten days. This is an ironic, and indeed embarrassing place for Courtney Love to have invoked the immediate and rabid compulsion to *be her*. Part of the job was already done because I was a singer, a certainty I arrived at really early, and that my mother responded to by sending me to singing lessons. Realistically, this was likely from a combination of genuine support and an astute anticipation of her own need to self-preserve. I'd been under the instruction of a man since I was eight who brought the strongest, most gorgeous voices out of young women by screaming hideous things at them. I learned to sing big, and loud, and impressively, because I was afraid of him. But abiding by fear produced results, and it is a strategy whose effectiveness has been difficult to abandon for healthier, if, truly, less dependable modes of productivity. I knew I was a singer, but I wanted blonde beautiful widow screamer. I wanted pain and glamor and volume.

The aforementioned embarrassment and irony of this experience derives from two main factors. First, it is embarrassing to admit that the Love I loved was the post-Hollywood, and if not quite post-, then certainly *less* rock version that emerged in 1998 with the album *Celebrity Skin;* the vain, yet bereaved, yet catchy follow-up to 1994's *Live Through This,* the vicious, maternal, grotesque bodily-reference-laden, but still tender as a bruise, and by all accounts superior predecessor, all the more appreciable for its refusal to be eclipsed by the suicide of Love's husband, Kurt Cobain, which happened a week before the album's release. There was no polish to *Live Through This*-era Love. The aesthetic was ultra-feminine, but budget and broken: vintage velvet baby-doll dresses with fraying hems and lace collars, messy red lipstick, Mary Jane flats, cheap tiaras, and her original nose. Sometimes an old satin slip. If there was glamor, it was decayed. By 1998 she had become the pristine excess that *Live Through This* had suggested the feminine didn't need to be. *Celebrity Skin*-era Courtney wasn't cool. She name-dropped (she name-dropped before too, but now she dropped Hollywood names), and talked about how great pilates is for your abs, and did pre-shows on MTV where she tried on dresses by Versace and Roberto Cavalli that she might wear to the music video awards. All her clothes were new. I couldn't see this then; what I saw was a rockstar that dressed like a movie star. And growing up in a small town, to a working-class, single mom, this was a glamor that precluded and seduced me. She had not completely lost her bite, it just all felt a little more bratty than commendably, genuinely driven by rage. You can see the shift in strange documents like the ads she did for Versace in 1998. There's a dash of fear in those pictures that asks if it's OK that she's there, or if she's doing it right. There's a first time-ness to her beauty, like she can't believe clothes that perfect even fit her. They were shot by Richard Avedon, whose famous images of Marilyn Monroe, blanked out in a sparkling evening gown, give away an exhaustion with the very performance of sex appeal and magnetism that Courtney is striving for in those 1998 portraits.

The second factor is that the all-female, feminist rock band Sleater-Kinney named themselves after the very road that I was driving on when Courtney got me. I'm from Olympia, Washington, the epicenter of the Riot Grrrl movement, branded as such in the 1990s with the emergence of feminist rock bands like Bikini Kill, Bratmobile, and Huggy Bear, many of whom released albums on Olympia labels like Kill Rock Stars and K Records. I did arrive at these bands, this feminism, other feminisms, other women in rock music, but Love was my gateway drug. I found 1994 Courtney through 1998 Courtney, which lead to early 1990s Courtney, Babes in Toyland, L7, PJ Harvey, then back down the Riot Grrrl rabbit hole, and further back into the recesses of feminist punk: X-Ray Spex, the Slits, Siouxsie and the Banshees, the Raincoats, Blondie, Patti Smith.

So, in order to become Courtney Love, I started taking guitar lessons, bought cheap versions of clothes that looked like hers, and bleached my hair. My dark auburn locks begged "Why" through the persistent shade of goldfish yellow that took several months to lift out. It looked dry and terrible, and I frequently glued craft store gems in my hair like Courtney had (probably by some more sophisticated means) in the *Celebrity Skin* video, which also didn't help. I spent a lot of time "practicing" in the mirror, rather than on my instrument. A year after discovering Hole, I arrived on my first day of high school a full-on clone, now verbalizing my intention to "BE-A-ROCK-STAR" as a way of normalizing and actualizing it. I told people I knew her, because it felt like I did, or could, and because teenagers lie. I hadn't previously considered where famous musicians came from. It was like they hatched out of an egg, or could be accepted as a fabricated invention because I mostly saw them on TV, like other fake things. The decision to try to be one, to assemble a band, write songs, was revelatory. My ambition was abject.

I was writing lyrics and vocal melodies, and my guitar teacher would help me with guitar parts and tab out chords for what I had written. He introduced me to some girls to play music with, but when the boy I'd had a year-long crush on — a fellow student council member, the person who introduced me to, and educated me about the (male) canon of punk rock, and took me to my first punk show at a divey Seattle all-ages club called the RKCNDY — asked me to sing for his band, I jumped ship.

Unlike other characters in this book, the memories I have of him could not capture who he is now because I have not known him in any significant capacity for over a decade. I am suspicious of the very anxious inclination I feel to protect him, but also feel it fair to acknowledge that these are the memories of, and about children.

X.

I forged my role as rock singer through a desire to live my idol's life. I was learning and developing through imitation. This left me susceptible to doubt, and the possibility that others might know better than me about how to *do my rock self* on, or off stage. I was fourteen when I started singing in the band, and fifteen when I finally got my band-mate Aaron to consider himself my boyfriend, even if that remained a fact socially unacknowledged for several years. He was older than me, and I thought he knew more about music, and everything else in the world than me. He is still the funniest person I have ever known, which derived in part from his gregarious presence and his extreme intelligence. Parlayed through willful exaggerations of sound and physicality, his comedic specialties were re-tellings of his absurd family dynamics, or teenage catastrophes that befell other teenagers: the time a round ball of shit fell from a basketball player's shorts during a layup, which he concealed by faking an injury, and smashing the shit into his knee as he clenched the joint in a performance of physical pain, OR the time his great grandmother willingly waited, trapped beneath a heavy table that she had assured her son (Aaron's grandfather) was unstable, so that he could see the result of his negligence for himself. The punchline was that she asked a young Isaac (Aaron's dad) to get her a piece of pickled herring while she waited. His humor and intelligence made it easier to forgive, or even rationalize the cruelty he was capable of. Like the man that taught me how to sing, I was also afraid of my first love and new teacher. I felt watched by him on stage, for all the mistakes I might make, for any mistakes I had made previously, that he didn't want me to make again. I recognize, but don't care, that he induced a paranoia disproportionate to real consequences. I know that on nights when I disappointed him, he was vocal about it, and that these criticisms destroyed me emotionally because I wanted him to think I was perfect. I developed a fear of him like the fear of being hit, something I would flinch against, or raise my hands to protect myself from. He never hit me, he was never going to hit me; but I perceived his disappointment as life-threatening. He was the main songwriter in the band. He wrote most of my words, and he demanded a certain kind of performance: "go apeshit." I never confronted him because I was afraid of being kicked out, first, and, a close second, I was afraid of us breaking up. I had no idea what I was worth to the band, or him, and this was reinforced by him telling me verbatim that I was replaceable. Actually, his words were, "Never forget how replaceable you are." I was encouraged to carry my insecurity around with me forever, checking in with it occasionally to prevent the unwarranted experience of self-worth.

I recently noticed on our first record that more lyrics than I remembered, though admittedly still very few, were mine. I would give him sheets of lyrics, and he would come back with some amalgamation of both of our words. I stopped giving him lyrics because, like live shows, it just felt like another creative space to leave wide open and vulnerable. On a rare occasion much later in our career, when I did attempt to contribute, the fear of rejection was actualized in sections of my notebook crossed out by him in a giant X so aggressively that he tore the page. Instead, I trusted my fear, and him. Aaron didn't know how to love me, and I didn't know how to maintain our relationship, or our band, other than by doing what he wanted.

When Aaron told me how he wanted me to perform it was simultaneously a permission and a challenge. Another performer through whom I had come to understand the allure of the seemingly possessed body — one that I thought Aaron was asking me to emulate — was Spencer Moody, who sang in the Seattle band the Murder City Devils. They played every few months, which made Spencer a more accessible object of study than Courtney in a pre-YouTube world. He put me in a hyper-vigilant state. Spencer pushed all his sweat and rage to the surface, then seemed to hold it, pressurize it with closed eyes and a fist clenched around a microphone, until he released his moxie, and sometimes his whole body into the audience. Those in attendance mimicked their leader. Limbs flew and surprised. We danced so hard. We left looking just-bathed. Once I saw him shimmy into the ceiling of a venue then called Graceland, and hang upside down from loose pipes, with the entire dirty, silver head of an SM58 microphone shoved into his mouth, screaming. Blood moved to the new base of his body, swelling his face into a wailing American Beauty. Sweat flooded his eyes like tears in reverse. A performer whose moves cannot be predicted by the audience, however, is different than a performer that is out of control of their body. And I started in the latter category. Originally I just spasmed. It was pure, though hollow experimentation that simply knew it could not be accused of lacking in effort. It was sexually useless.

X.

Antonin Artaud endowed the notion of "cruelty" with a romantic, transformative power historically reserved for love. He said it could devour darkness. He wrote that, "Everything that acts is a cruelty. It is upon this idea of extreme action, pushed beyond all limits, that theatre must be rebuilt."[1] Artaud promoted aggressive performances that shook their viewer from the complacent acceptance of the fictitious reality presented to them. Susan Sontag explained that Artaud conceived of performance as "an ordeal,"[2] and noted that members of the audience were not meant to "leave the theater 'intact' morally or emotionally."[3] Her words highlight that Artaud did not suggest physical, but rather psychological, or intellectual violence. He saw shock as a tool for cultural change, change in thought. The aesthetics used to employ those attacks might be unnatural, surreal, opulent, or even grotesque. This intention to provoke thought through radical invention and displacement is the backbone of subversion. It manifests in a myriad of visual ways.

Sexual subversion, however, was not one of Artaud's concerns. David A. Shafer, author of *Antonin Artaud* observes, "Artaud obsessed over sex. He suffered an almost pathological fear of sex."[4] Sontag affirms this:

Artaud regarded eroticism as something threatening, demonic. In "Art and Death" he describes "this preoccupation with sex which petrifies me and rips out my blood." Sexual organs multiply on a monstrous, Brobdingnagian scale and in menacingly hermaphrodite shapes in many of his writings; virginity is treated as a state of grace [...][5]

This obsessive fear of sex and eroticism noted by Shafer and Sontag draws significantly from Artaud's misogyny. Shafer points to the following excerpt from Artaud's collection of poems, *Nerve Scales*, as an example of his contempt for female sexuality:

Just like all women, you judge with your clitoris, not with your mind [...] Besides you have only ever judged me by my external appearance, like all women, like all idiots do, while my inner soul is the most damaged, the most ruined.[6]

His reference to women's judgement being sourced from their clitorides (yeah, that's the plural of clitoris — who knew), rather than their minds, both denigrates their sexuality and positions that sexuality as a threat to their intelligence. Two considerations must be drawn from Artaud's fearful relationship with sex, and the misogynistic attitude expressed above. First, though Artaud condemns sex, there is an irony at play in his promotion of provocative work that has the potential to produce feelings of discomfort that mirror his feelings toward sex. Given his own affected response to sexuality, sexual imagery would seem to represent the visual material most valuable to his approach. Second, sexually provocative feminist work should, by his own rationale, beat him at his own game — converting his misogyny to philogyny in some forced theatrical reckoning.

X.

I believe that the insecurities that were introduced to me through my creative and romantic partnership collected inside me in literal pools of thick black oil. When I was able to connect with this pain live, my performance changed. Burning through the horrible poison produced an ecstatic body more naturally, and without intellectual premeditation.

All of my love and all of my anger about not being loved moved my blood into shape. I spilled my guts. At our shows, I wept and wailed, and reached for the bodies that came to reach back at me. Eventually more bodies came, and more bodies came.

And this justified my love.

I found my space, my safety, my happiness, my power, through performance, effectively in that order. As I became sensitive to what felt good, and so good, and necessary, I learned control. I cannot separate, too, how the interior changes were mapped onto my exterior — how I tried to take ownership of myself from the outside in. I used surface to convey new security. I traded my jeans and band t-shirts for formal vintage dresses that I shredded up to the middle of my thigh. My hair was in a constant cycle of being bleached, dyed, or chopped into some new asymmetrical shape. When fans started to arrive at shows dressed like me, I questioned whether the traditional appeal of my decidedly feminine aesthetics of heavy makeup and costume dresses played into a regression, or at least an unprogressive stasis of women, by repeating trodden territory aligned with antiquated expectations of the female role (to be sweet, submissive, obedient, passive, demure, etc.). But, when this aesthetic was paired with our aggressive, angular music, and the confrontational and sexual performance it inspired from me — screaming, touching myself, often sweating my makeup into a mess, smearing it intentionally, writhing on the ground, or tearing parts of my dresses to allow for the types of movement on stage that might leave me bruised and sore — I found power in the destructive sacrifice of beauty and femininity. The actions and performance subverted the image. I would later contextualize the acting out of this refusal and the appropriation of these aesthetics through the work of performance theorists and queer and feminist discourse. This experience provided the most fundamental base upon which I built the research that appears later in this book. Though I had a confidence at my core that was produced by my mother's love and support, that confidence was tested by moving out of the predominantly male-less, small world in which I was raised. Performance renewed my access to self-possession, despite being utilized at a comparatively slower rate in my off-stage life.

X.

I broke up with Aaron just before my twentieth birthday, while we were on tour. The way I ended things was shitty and irresponsible, and I'm still sorry. I had fallen in love with our tour manager because he was kind and romantic. Owen. He got a tattoo of two red chairs I drew that were part of a set of flash cards I made to help him learn French. He held my hand when we walked down the street, which was new to me. He made me art things — sketches and collages and poems. It was a short-lived, if still extremely significant relationship. He was the first man to tell me I was beautiful, and the first, and only person to say to Aaron, "Don't talk to her like that." I know there's some precarity in here — that being told that you're beautiful isn't being told you're smart (which he did tell me also, all the time), and that women don't need men to rescue them. I know this now, and I knew this then, but I think my insecurity about coming off as needy — that adjective aligned by sexism with women whose totally rational needs are deemed irrational —prevented me from communicating when I wanted attention, or sex, or needed to have a conversation about why we loved each other, how we wanted to be treated, and other things we expected from our relationship. I had distilled these things down to unsophisticated sap, and it was a mistake highlighted to me by these first acts of praise and defense.

Ultimately we had to fire Owen because he got blotto in Toronto, and upon arriving at the hotel in Montreal around 3am, threw a suitcase full of our money and three of our passports into the woods. This was how he handled his feelings of jealousy after seeing me fix Aaron's hair. Our band-mate David had duct taped his passport to the interior of his suitcase per the advice of his girlfriend Esthere. They're married now.

X.

I wish I had learned the following things from my first relationship:

The love you have for someone must be separate and justified for different reasons than the reasons you may have for loving someone's art. Love for someone, and love for someone's art, are different.

When you collaborate with someone you love, do not mistake the love they give to your collaboration, what you make together, for love given only to you, in appreciation of what you are independently of your work.

You are not your work and must also love yourself independently of your work.

I have never again been afraid of a lover like I was of Aaron, but I did not continue to prioritize the kindness in my relationships that Owen had introduced to me in ours. My next big love was founded on chemical instinct, and it compounded what gratified me about performance with sex and video. Art again justified bad love.

X.

In *Camera Lucida* Roland Barthes says that, "Ultimately, Photography is subversive not when it frightens, repels, or even stigmatizes but when it is pensive, when it thinks."[7] Georges Bataille offers that, "subversion seeks immediately to create its own values in order to oppose established values."[8] As Barthes and Bataille suggest, subversion is an oppositional replacement of some traditionally established entity. Acts of subversion encourage us to think about the confines of what we know, and challenge those restrictions. As a mode of opposition and critique, I see subversion — by conventional definition, and as explored in the above quotes — as having a specifically generative or productive quality.

It is not the project of subversion to protest a problem through its direct enunciation or denunciation. Subversive images replace problematic ones gracefully and silently. They show the ease of dispelling traditional scripts and creating new roles. They demonstrate how quickly the repetition of the act can be interrupted. The power of what is being replaced is also effectively denied in this respect through its lack of acknowledgement.

X.

The first time I felt this thing is perhaps still the most staggering in my memory because it was so physical, and despite its abstract presentation, I was acutely aware of what it forecast. It was later though, when I met Ian, that it was most powerful, most crooked (unbelievable, impossible), instantaneously devoted.

It's a feeling as immediately and uniquely identifiable as getting a papercut, or being in water. In preparing this book, I found it described in similar ways throughout old diaries. My vision goes weird — like a dolly zoom shot in a movie. My whole body flashes into numbness. I feel too light. Sounds are muted, or sometimes tinnitus sets in. It tells me we will have sex, have complicated love, look at each other real close up. It only lasts a few seconds, but it produces a certainty despite how absurd the meeting circumstances might be. I have been with people despite their presence not eliciting this feeling, and I have been really confused when the feeling comes on, and my sentiments for the person are not in line with where it's telling me they will be. It's not an instant love; it's just instant confirmation that there will be love. And historically, a lot of pain. I wish it had happened with women, but it hasn't. I love women.

I once asked him over email if he remembered when we met, and his account had similar weight to it. He said,

"There was immediate non-verbal communication between us. It was intense and we didn't blink. But also felt like we could maybe start laughing hysterically at any point. It was intense and from that point on it felt like we couldn't stop staring. Does that sound about right?" I confirmed that it did, and that it was overwhelming. Then he asked me if I thought we had telepathy. I said, "Yeah."

X.

After seven years together our band got signed. Nabil Ayers put out our first two albums on his independent label, the Control Group, then took over managerial duties alongside Christian McKnight, who had more experience and connections with agents and promoters. We had slowly developed a devoted, mostly Seattle- and other small-towns-in-Washington-state-based following. During a tour for our second album, one of the openers had brought their friend along, a journalist from *Spin* magazine, Sarah "Ultragrrrl" Lewitinn. We stayed in touch with her after the tour ended because she had been releasing singles for bands with homemade packaging and wanted to put out one with us. I also just liked her. She was bright, funny, and brash without trying too hard. We had bonded over our love of Hole. She read my "Olympia" tattoo as a Hole reference, which it partly is. We didn't follow up with the initial request because Aaron and I were still dealing with the aftershocks of our breakup and he kept threatening to quit the band. We didn't know that she was putting a label together with Rob Stevenson, the A&R guy that signed the Killers, and that the label would be an imprint of the major label Island Def Jam. We were properly introduced to the new label, Stolen Transmission, at that year's South by Southwest festival (SXSW), where Rob and Sarah did a big showcase to launch it.

Following Sarah's introduction to him, we ended up on the packed patio of the launch party talking to Rob. He liked what he had heard, but alluded to us working with songwriters in the future and asked us if we were "in." Aaron wasn't into this, but navigated the whole thing with adequate tact. I think Aaron felt excited by the challenge of proving to Rob that we could make a record he wanted to sign without the help of his writing goons. We continued to tour throughout that summer, and the boys started writing the new record. Things between Aaron and I remained difficult and painful. I studied art history in college. "You know you're paying for that, right?" Aaron would ask whenever it came up. By autumn the record was done, and Aaron and I went to New York and took meetings with labels and Christian to "shop" the album. This is an awkward experience of watching someone with power listen to your music, and decide whether they are going to put some of that power at risk toward the possibility of gaining more power by making you successful. We had a couple of good meetings, including one with Rob and Sarah, but pressed on to SXSW again that year without a firm commitment from anyone to put the album out.

SXSW is a shitshow. There are too many people. It's too hot. Dusty. For those not at all prone to the subtle exercises of masochism which often signify devotion, it's an illogical misery. I am not that. I am still fairly unsure how to be proud of myself if there is not pain involved. I need receipts. In this regard, SXSW was my rapture. We played two or three shows a day, for several days. Remember the heat. Remember the thousands of bodies. Remember the booze, the ominous, confusing noise, the palpable industry bullshit, the sexism, the competition, and the expectations. Test me, please, so that I may relish in my validation through the observation of my own complicit, exhausted repetition. Believe me.

I was there to convince one person, and I did. I saw the very moment it happened, and this is the only moment from any show we played at the festival that has been recorded to memory.

My dress was a violet, 1950s evening gown that I had cut short. It was strapless, save a wide but delicate piece of tulle that ran over my right shoulder and diagonally across my back. At this show, there was a small, only slightly raised stage with a bannister around it. It was the kind where I had to pay additional attention to Aaron's instrument, lest he hit me in the head with it (as he had before (and as no one else in the band ever had)). During the slow buildup of one our song's bridges I climbed onto the railing, already blissfully flooded with adrenaline, and realized our low position had obscured how packed the bar's recesses were, how far back the bodies went, how many of them there were. I saw industry people scattered throughout the crowd. Now towering over everyone, and with the most hideous and certain grin, I looked down at Rob right as the chorus crashed down, and knew, "I got you."

That night another A&R guy from Epic, Pete Giberga, was desperately trying to get in touch with Nabil. He had taken one of the meetings with us in New York, but the live show freaked him out. It was 2am, and we were with Nabil when he answered Pete's call, and told him where we were. Not only did the guy track us down in the night, but when he turned up he could barely speak. He had lost his voice, and was imploring us through barely vibrating vocal chords to get in touch on Monday.

We eventually signed with Stolen Transmission about a month later, but the fact that Pete posed some competition gave us leverage, and the fact that he knew we were signing with Rob reverberated throughout the industry. All of a sudden we had buzz.

X.

We signed at the Universal offices in New York, then Rob
took us out for fancy Korean barbecue.

There was no disappointment to my dream coming true.
It was entirely perfect, and I felt overjoyed and sincerely
thankful at all times.

Enter: Ian.

X.

Just three months after SXSW, we were interviewing music video directors, and heading out on a tour with our new label-mates the Horrors. The tour started in Brooklyn, followed by a show in Manhattan, and a day off in the city before the next show in Boston. This gave us a couple days to come to the office and sort out promotion for the new record, which was due out three months later.

The Horrors had a very different kind of buzz than we did. Industry people thought teenagers would buy our music. Enough. The Horrors had a cult of Cool building around them that brought out beautiful young famous people, whose interest in the music was definitely secondary to the project of being in the orbit of its makers. Agyness Deyn was at the first show, which flipped my wig. She was a white-hot British model being touted as "the new Kate Moss." She was sat on some railing in the venue surrounded by a semi-circle of tall, thin people I attempted to recognize, and that I wondered how the hell I was going to impress. But I told myself I had to, that's what I was there for, that I had earned my place on that stage, and it wasn't time to be afraid of long legs. I considered who I might be in the relationship between mouse and elephant. Even the fame cloud that emanated off the Horrors directly was pretty intimidating. They felt unlike any of the bands we'd toured with before. Their aesthetic was deviant for the time, and bulletproof. They married prim tailoring and exaggerated accessories, derivative of 1960s English rock groups — blazers, waistcoats, trousers (all tight), oversized belt buckles, ostentatious bowed neck scarves , cravats — with a black-and-white palette, the occasional leather jacket, and the pointiest of leather boots with all manner of buckles on them that read of Sid Vicious or Lux Interior: Punk. Each of their hairstyles was its own defined shape. Tom, Reese, and Joe had sleek, short, Vidal Sassoon classics, and Faris and Josh ratted theirs up in big nests. They dressed like this off stage as well. They were committed, and like any good gang of icons (the Beatles, Spice Girls, Wu-Tang Clan), they each had their own identifiable brand within the brand. We had some nice moments with them over the course of the tour, and Tom and I would later end up being flatmates in London. But that first night they seemed evasive; subscribed to the Andy Warhol school of the bored and unimpressed. Their bodies hung inward, and their hair obscured their eyes, which made the simple assertion: Closed.

After the show I was taken around and introduced to label people as a new signee. The venue was packed, and I sank in amongst the bodies with my head down as we moved through to each introduction. Lauren Schneider, our publicist, kissed me on both cheeks with a, "Mwah! Mwah!," through which I could still detect the angle of a New York accent. She told me I was gonna be a star. She would. And yet despite its intense level of cliché this still does something seductive and hypnotic. Time freezes and you imagine a blue spotlight coming down on your smiling face, surrounded by glitter or rose petals. Head down, and we shuffled through the crowd again. We stopped at two sets of men's black shoes. I was wearing a short black shift dress with capped sleeves, and strappy, black vintage sandals with a low heel. I noticed my toes were turned in before raising my head, creating to me the image of a small child, ready to deliver its shame over a broken window or dead pet. I looked up and was introduced to two men that looked like twins; about the same height, both in all black. I still felt beneath a surface, looked at from above. Their faces seemed far away, without any light on them. I felt like prey, but of monetary rather than sexual, or other such value. They were music video directors, and we would have a meeting with them the following day at the office.

Going to the office was exciting because it confirmed "making it" as a rock band in a way that piss stops on tour in Montana and our still very low bank account balances really didn't. The day before the tour started we saw Usher arrive at the office just before we did, and met L.A. Reid, the chairman of the Island Def Jam Music Group. Reid remembered us as the band from the previous week's meeting about new artists. He liked the song that mentioned the devil. He pointed to us with an unlit cigar, a lascivious grin, and eyes wide open, and welcomed us to the label. He left to smoke that cigar with Usher, who Reid signed when Usher was fourteen.

When we came back the following day we were also introduced to the President of the label at the time, Jay-Z. His assistant let him know we were there, and showed us in. Two of the Horrors boys were with us, and took

Polaroids with him. He was quiet, but pleasant, more attractive, and seemingly also thinner in real life. I try not to wash the dress I met him in very often. I thought about the hand I shook having been inside Beyoncé.

Back at the Island office, the first couple of directors we met with weren't interesting to me. Our lyrics described images appropriate for horror movies, and I knew we presented like gothy, punk kids, but these guys missed all the genuine malaise, all the noir aesthetic, anything potentially lurid and nuanced, and skipped straight to comic book sci-fi aesthetics: green neon lights and ray guns and shit. At some point, I believe there was also a pitch involving some kind of sexy anarchist nurse. It was like I was invisible, and nobody filled these dudes in that our fans were a lot of young women and punked-out queer kids that wouldn't be seduced by some heteronormative cum shot in PVC. For me, there was no beauty, no intimacy, no art, no grace.

X.

Found: Actual, if edited (not changed, just reduced), original pitches written by people other than myself, printed without permission.

Treatment 1:

In an effort to eradicate their music forever, the authorities have been sent out on a "musical cleansing mission." The authorities will stop at nothing to exterminate all listeners. They must catch the band and give them shock treatments and a mental cleansing in an effort to go out and be poster children against their own music.

The band performs a regular concert. Suddenly, a group of doctors wearing masks and full scrubs walk into the audience, surrounding them. They take out chainsaws, weed whackers, hedge cutters, knives, and several other objects. Methodically, they travel through the audience, murdering everyone. Arms, skin, eyeballs, and body parts are seen tumbling amongst the crowd. Eventually, the doctors, whose suits are completely covered in blood, appear from both sides of the stage. They slowly walk towards the band. The doctors surround the band, gag them, and push them off the stage in stretchers.

Treatment 2:

Band is shot playing on the same stage as blood flies everywhere. Make it more PC, showing less of the visually appalling shots of the audience.

Ryann undergoes surgery. Ryann struggles to break free until she is heavily sedated. The Doctors are all wearing blonde Archie comic wigs with cut off sweaters. The nurses are all dressed like Betty with blonde wigs in pony tails. They give Ryann shock treatments and then undergo surgery involving small electric saws, giant scissors, and an assortment of anesthetics and cutting tools.

Eventually they remove the bandages, and Ryann is wearing a blonde wig and dressed exactly like the nurse (Betty). She has successfully been conformed to the authorities' look. They cart her off to a recovery room. Meanwhile, the dead fans at the concert start to rise. They get up and walk outside en route to the hospital. The gruesome fans bust into the hospital. They swarm the doctors in a feeding frenzy. Ryann rips her wig off, jumps out of the stretcher joining the band and finishes the song as her normal self, surrounded by blood-drenched fans.

Treatment 3:

Ryann, dressed in a 1950s-style dress, cowers in a corner. Three demonic human heads float around her (classic horror-movie-style). She closes her eyes, cries, and puts her hands over her ears trying to shut them out. Ryann wakes up on a floor. Suddenly, she is picked up and carried off by a shirtless, broad-chested giant with an evil grin on his face. She screams and beats him, trying to free herself from his grip. Her arms and legs are both tied with old rope. She looks up, and in terror she screams.

A nice man wearing a suit is arrives. He picks her off the table and comforts her. She is so glad to see him. She hugs him. The camera is tight on her face. We see the man's arms slowly pushing her down into a chair. The camera slowly pulls back. Clasps and arm restraints are put on her. A nurse puts her into her padded room. Ryann is living in a nightmare of insanity and delusions of grandeur.

X.

The meeting with Ian was different because he saw me. He knew me.

Now over ten years later I am plagued by the certainty and tenderness of our first meeting. I might translate these feelings as a commitment to forgive before anything bad happened. I could have been told then, that first hour, all the worst things he would do, and said OK. As they happened in real time they produced wounds and trauma that remained separate from the reserves of love I had for him. Love and pain were kept in their own accounts. Over time, each has been drained for want of deposits; sums effectively reduced by their own maintenance costs, and interest too weak to make the original investment grow.

The numbness set in. I felt possessed, and recognized these feelings mirrored in him across from me. As we spoke, I tried to ignore the slow and whispering, but insistent and incessant voice inside questioning whether I was going to marry this person.

We felt entirely separate from everyone in the room, to the extent that I remember turning away from him slowly, while he was still speaking to me, to see if what I was perceiving as so absurd, so inappropriate, could be confirmed by a look of obvious disapproval on anyone's face. It couldn't, which I laughed at, gently but audibly. I was forced back into the vacuous space to stare, and be stared at, and talk about music videos.

We discussed minimal, dark, feminine images. There was nothing else about his character that initially compelled me to him. He then suggested that perhaps his fiancé, an actress, could play one of the roles.

X.

We had spent the summer sending ideas back and forth for the video. It seemed to take trust to express what we hoped the other would agree was a strong image or scene. It was a forum for elaborating on what we found sexually compelling, attractive, beautiful; it was stimulating to explore what these things symbolized and meant to us. Aaron and I had been connected by the band that we loved, which heightened the intensity and stakes of our relationship, but what developed between Ian and I was a new experience of more evenly shared authorship and ownership. I felt that my creativity and perspectives were respected, and even enticing. Phone conversations lasted several hours. Part of the reason for this, however, was due to the pace at which he spoke. He has a strange, affected way. At several times during the conversations he would pause for five–nine whole seconds, before he continued his phrase with some completely unrevelatory word: "There was really something 1- 2- 3- 4- 5- 6-7- 8-9 NICE about the second Cure record 1-2-3-4-5 I mean the bass tones..." He would speak with abject sincerity about uncomplicated things. It's annoying. At the time I was mesmerized by trying to figure him out, but also sometimes found this absurd lack of self-awareness to its social deviance turn genuinely, impossibly hilarious. I thought there was more going on; that he was thoughtful, and that something about the slow approach made for a more nuanced reading. This is just one of the ways that I was wrong.

These conversations naturally expanded into discussions of our visual and sonic references which were inherent reflections of who we were. We were similar. Talking about Fellini, the Misfits, Sonic Youth, and RZA also helped obscure our age difference, and maintained the guise of a professional barrier as feasibly related to the project at hand. He was thirty-four, I was twenty-one. It is hard for me to reconcile the fact that I am still younger than he was when we met, and that I know that twenty-one-year-olds look to me like children, because it is the average age of my students. The connection I still remember as having a romantic and fated feeling to it, I have to recognize now as irresponsible at best, and more realistically, vaguely predatory. Even as I write this, as I wallow in its recollection, I must remind myself that this initial collaborative production of images that established how we would continue to communicate, to express desire for one another, and to know one another, has been my grossest misappraisal of what constitutes intimacy, trust, respect, and appreciation in a relationship. I clung to the feelings of validation and invention that were important to our working partnership, but these made opaque the project of identifying how recklessly I, and other women, were treated outside of it.

X.

Ian's fiancé was not cast in the video. I remember delicately suggesting that the inclusion of other actors might make it confusing for viewers to identify with band members. Really, the thought of not being the one in the front in our own music video felt like an unfathomable injustice, which is as mature of a way as I can find to translate the sound of a child's tantrum in my head, which more accurately captures what I recognize as my own sniveling vanity and entitlement. Or, maybe I am still really bad at conflating needs, wants, and earned rewards with shame.

The video originally centered around a large house with wild children, and a collection of strange objects that should present like those in the Mütter Museum — a medical museum in Philadelphia known for its array of beautifully displayed oddities, under glass, and in amongst red carpeting and golden banisters. Because the logistics of working with children were complicated, and because this idea bore noticeable similarities to the Yeah Yeah Yeah's *Y Control* video, it was changed. The new narrative revolved around a female cult, and a protagonist who sacrifices her tongue as initiation by cutting it out herself on the bank of a river. This was derived from one of Jonah's lyrics: "Take off your skin and dance with me. Cut out your tongue and sing for me."

Ian sometimes referred to the moment he first saw me in Seattle after a whole summer of calls and emails as our first kiss. This annoyed me, because I thought it was lazy, too cute. We filmed at Magnusson Park on Elliot Bay, a body of water that presents like a large, calm lake without much commercial traffic. Nuclear submarine fins, painted black, have been installed in an area of grass to look like an approaching pod of killer whales. Ian had gotten a bulky, industrial cart with equipment on it stuck in a narrow, grassy ditch with a well-camouflaged stream running at a shallow depth within it. He was awkwardly trying to undo the error of this move when I came down from the base area to say hi. While speaking, greeting me, he looked up and down, at me and the cart and back, without removing his hands from it, then scissored his legs wide across the ditch with sun in his eyes, seemingly compromising the strategic position that anchoring himself to either side might have afforded him. If this was our first kiss, then actually, it was fair presage of his ineptitudes with more advanced intimacies.

I was though, admittedly, so excited to see him. And to introduce him to Seattle, and to realize the project. The band posted a message online, and all our fans came out in black party clothes. They did interviews with Sarah about why they were there, and it was edited to seem like they were all running away with us. We all ate pizza together, and stayed late, getting cold, waiting for the right light, and thrashing around to the same backing track. The footage looked great, but there wasn't much else to it other than us bopping around in the dark. Ian suggested that I film additional scenes with him in Pennsylvania. The rationale was that he was from there, and knew where to shoot. The woods near his parents' house looked right — eerie, wiry, and strange — like Andrew Wyeth paintings, because Wyeth was born and died in the same area, Chadds Ford. We already had the performance footage with the whole band, so it would be cheaper just to send the singer to pick up shots of the narrative. I also think he wanted to see me again.

X.

I was experiencing a mental ricochet as the burning taste of artificial peppermint, the sensation of syrup dripping from my entire chin and neck, and the inability to feel my legs from the knee down competed for urgent resolution. There seemed to be less I could do about the curtain of gnats that had surrounded my face, because in the end I was still on their turf. Sometimes fake blood is given a flavor so that you know you can put it in your mouth. I was filling my mouth with it, and letting it drain out at a pace dictated by the relationship of its viscous, sticky composition with gravity. I was covered in this fake blood and real dirt, and the smell of the Brandywine Creek, a wide, swimmable tributary of the Christina River, where we had been filming for fourteen hours, for the second consecutive day. The smell was that of wet earth, with notes of the dead leaves or dead fish whose presence doesn't reveal itself until their micro particles are transported out of the water on your skin. We had collected scenes in the woods the night before, with altars made of wooden boxes, old black-and-white photographs, and candles. Women weaved slowly, threateningly, through the trees with full-length, burgundy and dark brown linen capes on, and stood in a circle as if preparing for a ritual. My cape was made of a simple, off-white net lace. I was filmed under fallen trees, or from behind spider webs, holding a bouquet of long, oily black feathers. These feathers also lined the simple rectangular box into which I was placed to float down the creek before arriving at a large group of boulders along the river's edge, where we were now filming the final scene. It had turned cold by the water, and I was wet, and shivering, and my legs had gone numb, which all helped inform the state of someone ready to cut out their tongue as a token of devotion.

I want to be clear that I never touched a camera in this process, but that these were the images — the minimal, dark, feminine images — whose design and meaning connected me to Ian, and whose continual creation I credit with sustaining that connection.

X.

He put ice cubes in white wine. Pennsylvania is hot in the summer. I watched his family, and don't remember saying much, but wanting to, wanting them to like me. His dad was cool and his mom was not; she had a shrill voice, and seemed uptight. Whenever I am in the presence of a couple who have been together for more than twenty years I imagine how they confronted their first infidelities. Was it explosive? Easy, and with tender resolve? I wonder. His parents' home was a place to leave equipment that had been driven in from New York. It was big, and had one of those too-nice living rooms that people only use on Christmas and Thanksgiving because they are otherwise afraid of ruining them, i.e. living. His youngest brother secretly grew pot in the backyard, which suggested to me that there were other familial things that were also hidden or unknown. I was offered a shower there while the crew unpacked, rather than waiting until I was back at my inn. He drove me home barefoot.

The Pennsbury Inn was typical of any East Coast country retreat, with a sweet, domestic interior, small rooms with quilts and fireplaces, and lush surroundings. He got out of the car to see the garden, which was lit by a huge moon as if it were day. A pale blue light hung above the black ground that stretched downhill toward a vanishing point, disappearing under trellises of roses that could be made out by their backlit, dark shapes, and their scent trapped in the unmoving summer air. I don't remember if he asked if he could see the room, or if I asked if he wanted to see the room. When we got upstairs we pressed our foreheads together, pausing to acknowledge and negotiate the collapse of several boundaries — to decide. I was laid out under white netting hung from a four-poster bed, and we kissed in a way that balanced the hyperbolic romance of the Inn, the garden, the moon, and the four months leading up to that moment, with the clear understanding that we were doing something wrong. We kissed only.

X.

The next day, Ian and I drove back to New York alone together in his car. We stopped in Philadelphia for cheesesteaks and sodas, which we ate while sat on the trunk.

He played Swervedriver and Ride. We talked about *Twin Peaks*, which I had not ever seen.

When we got back to the studio we kissed, and I hung on his body while we watched the footage, like he was my boyfriend. It was easy.

X.

What happened was that the distance between us produced conditions of extreme longing and extreme lust, to which I responded by producing — in collaboration with him, as directed by his desires, and by what I knew attracted him — images and videos of myself that a relationship with more readily available access to one another might not have inspired. I started making videos for my video director. I felt I had to offer something more, or entirely different than what a conventional relationship would. We reverted back to the creative dynamic we developed over the course of the video's production. What I made and what he directed was not your average pornography. These were performances, and they were accommodated by some of the still fairly new technologies that made them fast and feasible. Thank you, internet; thank you, camera phone; thank you, sexting.

Video: *Necklaces*

Five necklaces are tried on in succession. Clasps are opened gently for the camera, then re-joined carefully, behind the neck. The shot is tight, and close. Eyes go hard right, as if this helps to see the base of the neck. The camera is used as a mirror. Hair is pulled away from the collar area, and the necklace touched, grazed, or re-positioned. When hands are raised to remove the necklace the breast comes briefly into the frame. Editing is rapid, sometimes fixing on the eyes, blinking, the clavicle, the mouth, the fingers against metal, or pearl.

Video: *Legs*

The face is seen in three-quarter profile, backlit in front of a large industrial window. The view shifts to the front; the collar of a tight navy blue dress is being put in place. Hands smooth out creases in the dress, running down either side of the body, along the ribcage, hips, and outer thighs. A belt is cinched around the midline. Thigh-high net stockings are pulled over the knee in a rhythm dictated by the undulation of the wrists on either side of the leg. The shot returns to the face in profile, now nearly obscured by low light.

Photo Series: *Ribbons*

Eight images. A black satin dress is cut into long, wide ribbons, which are wrapped around a naked body in water. Three distinct lines are created across the breast, torso, and above the knees. The eyes are covered, and wrists are bound together. Exterior light cuts through a dark room in hazy panels that mirror the sections of fabric.

It would have been rational to think that I would never see him again after I left New York, and that I shouldn't, because he was engaged. He drove me to Penn Station where I took a train to the airport. As I got out of the car, the thought of never seeing him again smacked me in the chest and took my breath away. But, the certainty of that stupid, numb feeling I got when we met was still stuck in me like the stinger of a bee — itching, distracting, painful. I returned to Seattle at the end of August, and our band headed immediately back out on tour in the lead up to our album release, just a couple of weeks away. We would play New York twice before the end of the year. Ian and I became tethered by text messages, and sex messages, and tried to speak every day between soundcheck and the show.

When Ian and I saw each other we operated on a level of intimacy established by our correspondence and prolonged state of erotic tension. There was never an understanding of how we would function without the distance. The band passed through New York that winter, and seeing him produced scenes of a similarly cinematic, or unlikely, narrative quality as the videos I sent him because they were informed by limits. I was on tour, and shared hotel rooms with my bandmates. He lived with her. We were still operating under the pretense of sweetness, and uncertainty; a hotel room for the afternoon would have blemished all this. Our situation required greater creativity to navigate a lack of private space in which to fuck until we cried tears of cum. We made better use of touching and kissing than we might otherwise have had the patience for, given the option of penetration. We did this where two people who are more willing to compromise their dignity than their aesthetic sensibilities reasonably could. You start checking unalarmed doors in art museums and restaurants. You nearly fuck in the street. You discover that if you take the elevator to the top floor of the Bowery Hotel, then walk up the service stairs, there's an unlocked staff door to an unused part of the roof. There, on a cold night in autumn, you get pressed against the brick balcony that comes up to your chest, and your tits are splayed out on the rampart that scrapes your nipples before your face is pressed down ahead of them, and you watch your cold breath run sideways like cigarette smoke blurring out the tilted city. You feel a dripping wet mouth angle up the side of your throat and bite too hard on your earlobe while a hand presses hard against the inside of your thigh to spread your legs. You feel constantly watched because you are vigilant of being discovered, and this is as good as being in any performance. You want it to look right. You want to re-watch it on a loop. You cum on his hands.

Ian told me that he broke his engagement on an evening in January, not long after our affair had started. It didn't feel like a quick process at the time. The band was on tour, still, and had a night off. Ian and I met at Smith & Mills in Tribeca. It was new then, but I imagine it is still a cozy, dark, small room with scissor arm lamps and vintage prints around. There is a red globe light at the entrance in lieu of a sign.

I tried not to reveal my elation. He did not cast our relationship as cause, nor did he articulate plans for our future that might now be possible. Ian visited me in Seattle the next month, and we made love for the first time. He taught me to fuck slow, but couldn't be held at night. He had to fall asleep with the TV on, which I hated.

The fiancé never seemed real. Her existence created a constant, ominous, weight, threatening to remove him from my life. I had no animosity towards her, but could not access empathy for her either. I couldn't see her; I didn't know her name. I never once encouraged him to leave her, or used any verbiage about choice. I would imagine them tasting wedding cake samples together on a weekend when I didn't hear from him, and had resigned to the fact that we were temporary, and they were permanent. When I wasn't thinking about the engagement, I could remember that we didn't even live in the same place, and couldn't. The band was in Seattle, his studio was in New York. This began a practice that has become a compulsive habit, a useless ghost that wasn't threatening enough to exorcise. I process time according to my distance from New York City. We each had our own clock. If I was in Seattle I would count to myself, 10 (11, 12, 1). If in Chicago, 10 (11). The only time I tried to break things off though, was out of fear, not because of the logistics of space or time. I secluded myself in the women's bathroom at The Diamond Ballroom in Oklahoma City, and called to tell him I couldn't do it. I was surrounded by wall-to-wall 1950s sea-foam green tile. The cockroach slowly moving across the floor made me feel low and degenerate. I convinced myself his fiancé was a better woman than I was, and that I was making the right decision by forfeiting the relationship he'd eventually realize I wasn't good enough for. I called and initiated the process, which he rebuked. He said that the night before he'd had a dream that we were in the hospital, and I had just had our daughter. He said she had thick curls and was beautiful. I thought saying this to someone you didn't love was too sick. I thought he was telling me that this was what he wanted. He spoke with a gravity that contradicted the statement's recklessness, its tackiness, and my initial assumption that this was a sentiment recycled for its effective manipulation. I thought lying about something like this should make your teeth fall out and turn to ash. So it didn't end.

I would hope that the references I have hereto made about how wrong I was in my valuation of certain aspects of my relationship with Ian have conveyed regret, and in this way also served as apology (to her). And believe me, reader, you do not know from sorry just yet.

X.

A moment. This part doesn't belong to him.

Late August:
I returned from Pennsylvania.

September 1:
At a festival in our hometown we played a stadium, which held thousands of people.
I climbed high up the scaffolding at the side of the stage.
I stood along the crowd barricade.
This felt like my wedding and my funeral.
Then another tour.

September 16:
At the end of that small run, we flew from Salt Lake City to Seattle. Our tour manager drove across the country with our gear to meet us for the start of another tour on the East Coast, which would begin in four days.

September 17:
We went to a beach house in West Seattle rented by the radio station as a summer novelty. We talked about the record, and how we'd just flown in, and would soon be

flying out, and when the video would be released, and how happy we were, and it was heaven. We played an acoustic set at the record shop that Nabil owned. I was nervous about forgetting the words to one of the new songs, and cached some of the lyrics on the new releases board. The crowd was filled with people that had supported us for eight years, many of whom we had some singular significance to. We knew this because they would tell us, or write to us, or get tattoos of our lyrics, signatures, or album art, or cry with us. They made us real.

September 18:
Our third album was released on Stolen Transmission, a subsidiary of Island Def Jam. We played a sold-out release party at home.

November 30:
We were on tour, and had some time to kill before our evening show in Lancaster, Pennsylvania. We decided to spend our afternoon in Hershey, Pennsylvania, where Hershey's Chocolate is made. We'd heard the town smelled of chocolate, and it did. We drove down the main street, and all the lamp posts had on them large metal versions of Hershey's Kisses — the company's signature sweet — tilted at angles that suggested they were windblown and fancy-free. Kisses are bite-sized pieces of chocolate wrapped in silver foil with a thin ribbon of paper, labeled KISSES® in blue lettering protruding from their top. They are shaped like a tear drop with a flat bottom.

We arrived at the factory, and the factory had a ride. We were the only ones there. The ride involved a slow-moving cart that took us around a dark interior where animatronic cows and pastoral cartoon backdrops spelled out the story of Hershey's beginnings as a dairy farmer, and reinforced the secret of the chocolate's quality multiple times, in an over-excited voice: "It's all about the MILK!" I fact-checked this in my review of a YouTube video posted by a Hershey's enthusiast in 2010. The names, Olympia, Harmony, and Gabby were posted above fake stable stalls where we saw cow tails swaying joyously in unison. These cows then sang a jazzy number about "tasty treats" in a style akin to Tina Turner's rendition of "Proud Mary." Things got a bit dry during the unnecessarily methodical explanations of the factory processes, but soon we were spat out into a wonderland of conveyor belts, overloaded with Reese's Peanut Butter Cups, York Peppermint Patties, Almond Joys, Kit Kats, and the like. The ride's narrator concluded by saying, "Our goal at Hershey's is to keep you smiling. Because bringing happiness to you is what we're all about."

As we left the ride we were given promotional packets of a new candy-coated miniature Kiss. We joked about the ride as we exited down a long ramp, and Aaron answered a call from Nabil. He began chewing on his hair, which he did when he was nervous or thinking. He asked flatly, "What does that mean?" Rob, the man that signed us and ran our label, had been fired. No one knew what it meant.

X.

We weren't given answers. Sarah had been fired too, and Stolen Transmission no longer existed. We were owed nothing by our parent label.

We kept touring on an album whose promotion had been abandoned. We didn't have other contacts at the label. We didn't know who to call. We kept being re-assured by Rob that everything was going to be "OK," and for him only, it was. He got another high-level A&R job. He is currently the Executive Vice President of Republic Records, another division of Universal. He said he would re-sign us and never did. Contact dissipated over a year of waiting.

Our bandmates Scott and David both had partners that they had been with for several years — exceptional women — from whom they were perpetually separated by tour, and to whom, luckily, they are now married, probably because for the first time they chose these women over the band, at times that represented their last chance to do so.

After several label-less tours that were not bad, but pointed to no clear advance in our careers, Scott called a band meeting in a badly-decorated hotel room in Dallas, Texas, with baby blue shag carpeting, and quit. David eventually followed.

X.

When I visited Ian in New York we stayed at hotels, and he paid in cash.

He said she still had things at the apartment they had shared and was worried about her coming over when I was there. She still had a key.

Doesn't explain the cash, does it.

A suitcase full of black lingerie, and heels that never leave the room. Spit. Consensual force. Swollen lips. Marks made on the skin. You come into me, and you stay. The weight of you, and the size of you press me into silence, and submission, and forgiveness; and you fill me up with a poisonous gift that feels like trust. You put this in me. So now what, so now what?

X.

Through music video, Madonna put dark sex and dark love into pop music and the popular landscape at large. She was one of the first. And whereas something like the early erotic masochism of Nine Inch Nails' *Happiness in Slavery* might have been expected from them, because their music was also dark, Madonna's aesthetics permanently changed pop. She explored music video's ability to shock, not just through enticing, accepted sexual imagery, but also through unexpected iterations of unconventional sexual representations that challenged heteronormative standards — S&M, queer love, pain.

I have chosen to consider Madonna's videos for *Vogue*, *Justify My Love*, and *Erotica* as a connected series — a triptych — produced during her most controversial period. The videos share a dramatic black-and-white aesthetic, queer and sexual themes, and become progressively more explicit.

The first of the series to be released in 1990, *Vogue*, directed by David Fincher, envelops Madonna in a queer world marked by rampant Voguing, ostentatious glamor, androgyny, and women, including Madonna, appropriating traditionally male dress. Reinforcing this queerness are the aesthetic similarities to a Robert Mapplethorpe series — the high contrast and classical handling of idealized bodies that might be found in his *X Portfolio*. In the opening sequence, men and women in suits are positioned next to sculptures and paintings, suggesting their parity — hardness, beauty, mastery — untouchable. The figures are put in motion by a pulsing beat. Madonna whips out her black, velvet-covered cone tits, and by the end dress shirts are turned into white flashing spirals with the aid of an intense wind fan. It's not without its humor, or its acknowledgements of these absurd exaggerations of the power of the exterior. But the characters drip with a confidence, justified in each delicate, gliding, committed motion, that tells us they know they are beautiful. And whether they are or not, or always were or not, this conviction, this decision to know, has made them free. Madonna calls us superstars, it does something to us, and we are offered that same freedom, "black or white," "boy or girl," on the dancefloor. You HAVE to Vogue.

Before I proceed, let's acknowledge that Madonna has been heavily critiqued as having appropriated Voguing from the New York ballroom scene. In her chapter in *The Madonna Connection,* Lisa Henderson implies that Madonna's appropriations are beneficial to her in terms of aligning herself with queer culture, but that this may only be legible to those in said culture.[9] For those in her audience unfamiliar with the gay ballroom cultures Madonna is referencing, or arguably elevating to mainstream visibility, the queer elements of her work go unannounced, presumably to avoid evasion of her heterosexual fan base. Though a fair argument, I do not read Madonna's actions as Henderon does. Henderson suggests that Voguing has been incorporated as queer novelty, when in fact much of Madonna's career has been marked, not just by queer aesthetics, but by queer acts, language, and activism. This is evidenced by the queer world Madonna continues to build throughout the triptych.

Justify My Love, also released in 1990, directed by Jean-Baptiste Mondino, depicts dream-like sexual encounters in a hotel. It was shot at the Hotel Royal Monceau in Paris. Mondino has said, "I did an experience. The whole idea was to lock ourselves into this hotel for three days and two nights. Without any rules […] Nobody was allowed to go out."[10] He shot without a script, and said by the end of it he was unable to differentiate the real from the performed. In the video, Madonna stumbles through the bleached halls of the hotel, holding the back of her hand to her head, exhausted. She carries an old-fashioned suitcase. Its weight tilts her frame. She wears a black trench-coat and heels. She passes an androgynous figure who waits in an open doorway, topless, with breasts covered by a decorative 1920s sheath and several long strands of pearls. The camera quickly passes a splintered view of a wiry, shirtless man looking down, as if observing himself being blown. Madonna drops the suitcase, leans against the wall, and runs her hands up her temples, and down the length of her body, before kneeling to the floor. The trench-coat falls back, showing the garter belts running up the length of her uncovered thighs. The camera moves low, at the level of her knees, which are bent, splayed in opposite directions. Her hands grope at her black underwear, and our view moves within her legs, then in tandem with her body — up toward the man that has arrived in the hall, watching her. Figures in lingerie, a dancer in a black bodysuit with claws obscure gender identities in the wash of fantasy and eroticism. We are returned to Madonna, who is now in a bedroom, slowly removing her clothes, displaying herself on the white bed. The man that lays on her is not the figure we see kissing her as the shot pulls away. The sex of the new character is at first indeterminable. They have eyeshadow on, sharp features, a feminine face. They, and Madonna, are watched by a male voyeur at the side of the bed. As the camera scrolls down the length of their bodies pressed together, the figure is revealed to be a woman. The character is played by a model, Amanda Cazalet, who was courted by Madonna off set, through love letters that were eventually sold at auction in 2018. Two trans-women caress each other's faces tenderly, while observing themselves in a mirror.

This scene is followed by, what is beyond a doubt, the representation of penetrative fucking. You may think there's a lot of fucking in music videos, but really, there's not. There are sexualized bodies, but they don't fuck. This is a radical moment Madge is pulling off. Marilyn Manson includes fucking in his videos, but he doesn't get there until 2004, in the Asia Argento-directed video, *(s)Aint*, later followed by fucking in 2007's *Heart Shaped Glasses*, and 2017's *Kill4You*. Fucking is included in Flying Lotus' *Parisian Goldfish*, in 2008, and there is digitized, faceless fucking in Björk's *Pagan Poetry*, released in 2001. The Prodigy's *Smack My Bitch Up* is perhaps *Justify*'s closest competitor, which includes an excellent lesbian fucking scene — excellent for its certainty rather than suggestion — though this is released seven years after Madonna first fucks on camera. Other queer figures appear, including a butch woman in a cop hat, whose suspenders cover her nipples. She taunts one of Madonna's lovers, who has been put in a latticed leather harness, with his hands tied behind him. Women in drag draw thin mustaches on each other and gaze into the camera. Madonna leaves the hotel hurriedly, with suitcase back in hand, and her lover still reaching out for her to return. She throws her head back as she laughs, with mouth open wide, then bites her knuckle. The video fades to black, and a quote appears against the screen: "Poor is the man whose pleasures depend on the permission of another."

Despite how the video translates in the above formal analysis, another of Lisa Henderson's criticisms is that the queerness of the sex scenes in *Justify My Love* is too ambiguous to be effectively confrontational.[11] Rather than any ambiguity in its depiction of queerness, how I interpret the restraint Henderson identifies is more as a strategy to build eroticism throughout the triptych — naturally peaking in *Erotica*. She also compromises the strength of her argument somewhat by considering the absence of any queer representation in the vast majority of music videos at the time. She says, "*Justify My Love* defies some of music video's worst clichés and opens up an aesthetic and political corner for other ways of envisioning sex in popular culture."[12] In this way, Henderson asserts that Madonna sanctifies new visions of sexuality by pushing the standards of the music video genre.

There is further contradiction in Henderson's argument, as she proceeds to criticize Madonna's construction of an environment where that sexual agency is explored. Henderson negatively describes the hotel where the video takes place as a venue where the sale of sexual services has long benefitted men and subjugated women as sexual and economic property.[13] This quote is somewhat troubling for its totalizing condemnation of female sex work, without even the interrogation of possible agency. Also, this assessment is predicated upon a fictional narrative, where Madonna plays a character — a prostitute, by Henderson's reading. I would like to suggest the alternate reading that Madonna Louise Ciccone is playing *Madonna* — developing the provocative persona used to market herself, and servicing a queer feminist politics at risk during the conservative climate at the time of the video's release. This reading positions Madonna as the one in control and reveals her agency, rather than reading her performance as a submission to the desires of the man that Henderson suggests has hired her character.

Madonna's *Erotica*, directed by Fabien Baron and released in 1992, expands and proliferates the queer and explicit images in *Justify My Love*. We see Madonna in the opening shot, masked, behind a shimmering, metallic curtain. The following shot shows Madonna in lingerie, straddling a male figure, seated in a chair in a masculine study. The two kiss, and disrobe each other, before the scene fades back again to the shimmering curtain where the word "Erotica" scrolls across the screen. A full body shot of Madonna shows her, still masked, wearing a man's tie, with a whip in hand. Her short blond hair is slicked back, and she appears as an androgynous dominatrix. Within the first seconds of the video, Madonna has destabilized gender norms, adopted a masculine dress while dominating her male lovers, and established an intensely theatrical sexual landscape. She renders us creeps and voyeurs (inclusionary and accepted roles in the already scandalous world in which we are immersed), compelled to watch the taboo scenes for their inherent eroticism and rich images.

The dark aesthetic of the video reflects the stereotypically "bad" or "sinful" connotation of sexual fantasy, and queer sex, more pointedly. The consistent glamorization of the characters, however, subverts those negative connotations, while acknowledging a separation from convention through lurid imagery. Madonna theatricalizes something of the totality of sexuality, including drag, bondage, role-play, homosexual, and group sexual encounters. Though the scenes and aesthetics signal the deviant nature of her subjects, Madonna unveils honest facets of sexuality, rarely seen in mainstream media. She elevates and legitimizes these truths and fantasies through her extreme visibility and success.

Images flash of Madonna with a whip in her mouth, smiling subversively into the camera, implying that she will derive pleasure from its sadistic use. A feminine, muscular male dancer is shown pressing himself up against a mirror with cigarette in hand — his masculine appearance subverted by his unexpected vanity and grace. A couple in formal dress watch the male dancer, whose movement is sped up and distorted, before they kiss in the audience. Madonna is shown kissing the model Isabella Rossellini, the male figure from the opening scene, and a butch woman with a shaved head. Another supermodel, Naomi Campbell, appears behind Madonna, grabbing her body while looking into the camera in a provocative motion of sexual possession. Madonna reaches her arm behind her, grabbing Campbell around the neck, as we see her twist her head and push her tongue out toward Campbell's mouth. These exchanges with Rossellini and Campbell again reinforce the queer current of the video, particularly subversive given that, as models, these women represent classic objects of desire for heterosexual men.

In the following scenes, Madonna is shown pouring hot wax over the chest of a man, whose arms have been tied above his head. The woman with the shaved head is shown with a doppelgänger and Madonna on a mattress, with rope lying next to it. The woman is shown again, standing over a kneeling Madonna, prying Madonna's jaw open in front of her pelvis. Madonna puts on a leather mask, and kneels on her hands and knees in a bondage apparatus that allows a man to bridle her like a horse, hold the reigns attached to its metal loops, and straddle her back

The muscular male figure also wears a leather bondage harness. The scene changes, presenting her in an evening gown, assuming the dominant role, again with the whip, holding reigns linked to what appears to be a dozen nude male bodies. Madonna changes into yet another S&M-style costume with a leather biking cap and chaps. She dons a punk-style, spiked collar, held to the wall behind her with heavy metal chains. In a frontal shot she looks directly into the camera from her restricted position, rolling her tongue around the edge of her mouth, as if declaring her ability to sexually provoke despite having assumed a submissive position.

Another subversive pairing Madonna includes is a scene in her evening gown where she sits on the lap of man, presumably in his seventies, who touches her body and face. She has assumed the position of a call girl, although given the various positions of power she has adopted throughout the video, it is unclear to what extent she is truly at the man's service, or simply playing yet another role wherein sexual power is exchanged and explored. The words "I'll teach you how to" are shown on screen, concluding with an image of Madonna waving her finger in denial at the camera, as the word "Sex" appears. The video concludes with a shot of Madonna hitchhiking naked in Miami, Florida.

Madonna elicits shock and sexual arousal by exposing and relishing in the proclivities usually kept hidden, or secret, for their deviations from heteronormative desire, for their very expression of a love and fascination with sex; its physical and aesthetic limits. She exposes the performative nature of sex: the numerous costumes — leather masks, whips, chains, etc., as well as choreographed exchanges of dominant and submissive roles, which in turn highlights the agency offered by performance to subvert normative standards.

Erotica delivers the affirmation of same-sex encounters, which Henderson critiques *Justify My Love* for representing less explicitly. The various issues of queer representation that Henderson delves into are the same sites I recognize as valuable subversions of gender norms inserted in the landscape of the popular. I find this achieved not just through the sexually provocative nature of Madonna's own identity, but through the complex performances she stages in video, where queer culture is elevated and sanctified, and binaries destroyed through same-sex encounters and experiments in subcultural role play. Rather than attempts at queer appropriation, these videos operate more ostensibly as Madonna's own self-exposure as queer.

X.

Not long after Scott quit the band, I was at a party with my best friend Caitlin. We had been introduced to Mark Gajadhar, the drummer for Seattle band the Blood Brothers. They were a frenetic post-hardcore group, with two singers and a bombastic live show that seemed to be a precedent for northwest bands at the time. They had a cult-like local following, but they had also established a sturdy national and international fan-base. They were a big deal. Mark was/is an incredible drummer, and had started making beats for a hip-hop project on the side called Champagne Champagne. Caitlin and I were joking to him about our new synth-pop band, where we sang about bicycles and the library. Thinking we were serious, he offered to make us beats if we ever needed any. This was the first time I had ever thought about working with anyone other than my bandmates, or about making pop music. It was the first time I even considered how pop music was made. Of course — beats. I confessed to Mark that my project with Caitlin was not real, but that if he wanted to work on something together, we could.

We started meeting weekly. Mark would send me several tracks, and

I COULD DO

WHATEVER

THE FUCK I

WANTED TO

WITH THEM.

X.

Mark gave me total freedom. He trusted me. I played his tracks on repeat and wrote to them by silently committing vocal melodies to memory while sitting for hours at the Herkimer coffee shop in Seattle's U-District. I had mostly sent him Madonna references from *Confessions on a Dance Floor* and *Hard Candy*. I know these aren't her best jams, but I liked the disco sounds, the minor liberties taken against her more classic pop structures, and the unexpected palette of overly bubbly, happy synth sounds that were used when the Neptunes, Timbaland, and Justin Timberlake produced her. Say what you will, it's no *Like a Prayer*, but I also liked the very human sentiments of insecurity that are all over *Hard Candy*, and that spoke to my particular concerns around the production of longing from a distance: "She's not me," "You always love me more, miles away," "I need to go back there before it's too late." Mark had complimented this by sending me Glass Candy and Chromatics tracks, both produced by Johnny Jewel. It all worked. Our choruses repeated, and were catchy, but were set within electronic textures that were dissonant to commercial pop sounds. Sometimes they were dark and sinister, sometimes dancy, warmer. Sometimes I screamed. One song was a waltz, with me singing in French to an organ. I was never told that anything was bad, or that I was bad, or that I should do something differently. I also never, ever, not once, got the impression that Mark was interested in me sexually. He had a girlfriend, they had a cat and dog, and we could collaborate, bringing both of our talents to share, without this having any bearing on our hearts.

Aaron identified the threat in this, and tried to render the situation by expressing his own desire to make pop music together. He immediately made all the wrong moves. We had one practice. He spoke authoritatively about how often we should meet, and that we should complete one song every practice. His words were choppy and intimidating, accentuated by a chopping motion with one hand landing into the flattened palm of the other. I hated all of this. It made me as sick and scared as it ever had.

The other value of working with Mark was that he didn't care that I wrote about Ian. Aaron was still sensitive about our breakup, three years after it happened. I'm not degrading this by the way. The whole thing was terrible and confusing for a long time. I missed him as my boyfriend, frequently. I didn't feel comfortable with him knowing I was seeing anyone, let alone our video director, and certainly didn't want to share my lyrics about it with him. Ian's contact had been decreasing at what was first an imperceptible rate. I missed him all the time, and writing about it when the other great love of my life, our band, was also in a state of uncertainty, felt urgently necessary. We weren't performing much, and I had no way of exercising my congestions of panic and fear. By the time I recognized Ian's retreat, I was too proud to fight for him.

My experience working with Mark destroyed all my

paradigms. It turned out, given a completely basic level of autonomy, I could write, make, feel, be, and that this was not contingent upon sharing love and sex. Not only would I write songs then, but I would make videos and images that weren't for Ian, and begin the process of cultivating in myself the knowledge of film that was also a significant aspect of what attracted me to him. Mark and I called our project WEEKEND, after the Jean-Luc Godard movie. When Champagne Champagne started doing well, and he needed to turn focus to it, he said I was welcome to have, release, and perform the songs, as long as he was credited, which he always was. From this point, I started performing as Ryann.

X.

Bertolt Brecht's signature "epic theater" was, above all, aware of itself as theater. He maintained, "It is most important that one of the main features of the ordinary theatre should be excluded from [epic theater]; the engendering of illusion."[14] His aim was to acknowledge and expose the construction of a performance, without sacrificing intellectual engagement and meaning. Rather than identifying with characters through a fictional narrative, performers could be used to communicate abstract ideas or social commentary through bodily sign and symbol. Many of the videos in this book expose gender as performance through their extreme and unconventional gendered representations. By exposing the manipulation of gender at an extreme level, common iterations of gender performance also come into view. Walter Benjamin echoes how Brecht's strategy might be applied to this effect in *Understanding Brecht*. He says, "Epic theatre, then, does not reproduce conditions but, rather, reveals them. This uncovering of conditions is brought about through processes being interrupted."[15] In the context of these videos, what is interrupted is the "stylized repetition of acts" — to draw from Judith Butler — which conventionally establish gender identities.

The modes of interruption performed in the videos

explored in this book also frequently produce critical distance — a strategy written into the epic theater. While Artaud focused on shock and spectacle to awaken his viewer and produce thought, Brecht's strategy toward similar aims proposed a loss of empathy. Originally adapted from Chinese theater, the "alienation effect" or "distancing effect" — "*Verfremdungseffekt*" in Brecht's tongue — prevents the viewer from submitting to an experience uncritically (and without practical consequences) by means of simple empathy with the characters in a play. Brecht's productions put their subject matter through a process of alienation — "the alienation that is necessary to all understanding" — as Benjamin put it.[16] Through an independence from empathy, he sought to develop an audience's consciousness.

X.

Music Video: *All Yours*

The word "Sound" is embossed in a brass plate below an elevator call button. The hand that reaches out to press it is wearing black, leather, fingerless gloves. The music begins and we watch the numbered floors pass from inside the vintage elevator — 2, 3, 4 — our view blocked by its large metal gate, which secures us inside. A close-up of a woman's face, with black makeup smeared across her eyes like a mask. Two people, seen in profile, face each other. The shot is tight, from cheek to neck; their proportions, the curves of their features nearly identical. Their lips are parted slightly. Images shift on the beat. An androgynous figure leans in to kiss the first woman seen. She is gently bitten, and her lower lip pulled away in the teeth of the figure that has been revealed to be a woman with short hair. Images of the women from their waists down, holding each other's thighs, shift to the view of floors still ascending through the gate of the elevator. The elevator stops, the women kiss. In strobing light, a surreal sequence begins. A woman licks the length of her wrist and hand, which is covered in glitter, penetrating her mouth with her metallic-coated fingers. The glitter left in her mouth is dragged down her tongue and the length of her neck, which sticks with saliva. The camera disappears into her dark, sparkling mouth, and the footage is edited to flash with the beat before the music softens at the bridge.

X.

Our band didn't recover. We lost our label, then Scott, then David, and couldn't recoup on morale. We decided to end it with the intention of Aaron and I continuing with new members under a new name after the breakup. Scott and David returned for the last show. I started having panic attacks in my car in the month leading up to it. They began with delicate tears, usually while paused at red lights, but within moments possessed my respiratory system, and I hyperventilated, too fast, too heavy, a failing machine. Death was coming. For our funeral, I chose a pristine 1950s evening gown, made of heavy ocean blue satin with slivers of metallic stitching across the chest in an abstract floral pattern. It hung from a hangar on the outside of my closet for weeks, and I stared at it from bed, trying to fully grasp the end of things. If I woke briefly in the night, I would be alarmed into an upright position, having mistaken its dark shape against the white door for a ghost. I didn't move it. I accepted that, in a little while, it would essentially be one.

X.

The last show was a purity.

It was all for you.

X.

I was at first excited to start afresh with the new lineup, the new band, but old dynamics revealed themselves that I was not prepared to commit another decade to navigating. I hate that I don't remember the details of what it was about at that particular time, but since Aaron only ever made me cry by telling me how disappointing I was to him, we can assume that waiting in the vocal booth for the muscles in my throat to relax and my sinuses to clear so that I could record vocals on the new band's demos had been initiated by some critique of my vocal delivery, or timing, that would also have been very deftly linked by him to flaws of my person — selfishness, laziness — that might have been the real source of these musical errors... "If you had practiced more," "If you cared," "If you weren't so busy with your other projects," etc. I took my headphones off and tried to gather myself to avoid one of these new, unpredictable invasions to my lungs that I was only considering a detriment in terms of what other insults they would arm Aaron with ("Don't be so dramatic." "Do you know how much time this is wasting?" "Do you know what this costs us?"). I asked myself why I was doing this. Standing there after the death of our band, without any obligations or reinforcements, the fair question arose.

It was not rhetorical; I demanded an answer from myself. I felt the most blissful, calming, relief when I heard the truth, still there after over ten years: I am doing this for Jonah, because I love him.

The fact that I could separate my own self-interest, in fact that I could see that there was no self-interest there, gave me some ability to consciously give myself to him in spite of his cruelty, and to enjoy it, rather than feeling, as I had the entire time, that I should be grateful to him for allowing me to be there — replaceable as I was. I loved him because we had made a thing together that had defined my adult life, and that I loved most. I loved him because he showed me things that shaped my identity and brought me immense joy. But it also became clear to me that my love need not be expressed as his instrument. A month later I told him that I was going to move to New York for my master's degree. I offered to fly back and forth. Classes would be in session for less than nine months, and there were significant breaks for holidays. He didn't go for it. In ten years, I hadn't been away from him for more than two weeks. When I left, he scrapped all the songs we had been working on rather than getting someone new to sing them.

Distance and lies were what dissolved my romantic relationship with Ian. There was nothing that my erotic homemade cinema could do about it. It ended on a work trip to New York I took with my boss — a bar and restaurant owner I'd had to start assisting when we stopped touring to write new songs. He said he was in Pennsylvania filming, and would return the morning my flight left. He suggested I meet him at his studio at 4am. I was hauling an impractical, cherry red 1960s Samsonite suitcase around by hand because I loved it. I remember literally muttering to myself how stupid this all was — the meeting, the suitcase, the time — as I marched out to get a taxi, hands cramped and body off-kilter. I justified my decision with the idea of breaking up in person.

He met me outside and escorted me up, which meant we had to be in the elevator together. The elevator was so beautiful. Square. Enticing geometry. Industrial size, eleven feet or more in each direction. Metal. He pulled the emergency stop. I saw the blurred reflection of my red case in the ceiling and thought of the red globe light outside Smith & Mills. I wondered what other benign and unrelated objects would remind me of him for the rest of my life. In the elevator we remembered our love through the attachment of our mouths to other wet parts of our bodies. We forgot the traumatic mourning rituals that had come with every other one of our separations since the first. We fed.

We eventually made an awkward move to the studio, having already exercised our communion, but feeling the irony of needing to speak about the silence established in recent months. The sun hadn't yet come up. The space was dark, with one warm frosted light glowing in the corner. I spilled a glass of red wine, which made me feel like a child; dumb and messy. I was placed at the edge of a chair, told to hold its outer back edges, and spread my legs wide. I watched hands disappear under my skirt and felt them inside of me. I felt dizzy and sad, and closed my legs gently around his face causing him to reverse. I used language learned from films. I can't do this. What's going on. Say it. And then he said he couldn't be in a relationship, with me, right now. He called me a taxi, and before I got in he told me to call when I arrived. I exploded, yelling that I would never call him.

X.

I moved to New York that summer. I was going to start classes in the autumn. I was going to take the songs I had made with Mark and become Madonna while I still could. I admit that part of me was also there to get him back. To try.

I was allowed to stay at my Seattle boss' studio apartment in London Terrace, one of the oldest, grandest apartment blocks in New York City, and at the time, and probably still, the home of Debbie Harry. I saw her once; she still wears leather and sunglasses. I lived on toast with peanut butter, coffee, and the staff meals provided at the Ace Hotel, where I got a job. I had to figure out how to get first, last, and deposit for a room of my own.

I accepted a job as a dominatrix at a place that was conveyed to me as actually having quite a boring, older, conservative clientele of mid-town business men. I never started because I couldn't afford the costumes and the hours conflicted with my two-week training doing the overnights at the hotel. I also cleaned some creep's apartment dressed like a French maid for $40 an hour. I felt sorry for myself, and collapsed punishment of those feelings with the comforting position re-assuming the sexual gaze of easy targets.

X.

Judith Butler maintains that gender is a kind of imitation for which there is no original.[17] Our big mistake then, is thinking that our sex is supposed to dictate our gender identity. According to her, the act of gender is what produces its meaning.

Butler thereby argues that gender is performative. She differentiates this from gender's theatricality by saying, "Performativity must be understood not as a singular or deliberate 'act,' but, rather, as the reiterative and citational practice by which discourse produces the effects that it names."[18] This quote from *Bodies That Matter: On the Discursive Limits of Sex* clarifies that gender is constituted in its very determination, before its performance begins. Just by calling someone a girl *over* and *over*, the label itself *does* something to the person. The naming, and the acceptance that we are what we are being called informs our understanding of how we are expected to act.

Like gender, she also says sexuality is unstable, and that heterosexuality is repeated out of compulsion, and the necessity to confirm that it is the natural standard (when it's totally not).

Butler attributes the production of the gender binary to a normalization of heterosexuality. She says, "the heterosexualisation of desire requires and institutes the production of discrete and asymmetrical oppositions between 'feminine' and 'masculine,' where these are understood as expressive attributes of 'male' and 'female.'"[19] These "expressive attributes" of masculinity and femininity perpetuate a heterosexual model that procreation has been falsely framed as relying on (procreation has proven entirely sustainable, even when desire between those procreating is absent, i.e. artificial insemination). This hetero-sexist structure reaffirms itself through gender's performative effect, which Butler describes as a repeated ritual; a culturally sustained temporal duration that we call "body."[20]

She also questions how this system may be destabilized; how to fabricate gender in terms which reveal every claim to the origin, the inner, the true, and the real as nothing other than the effects of drag.[21] Like Artaud (but without the misogyny) and Brecht she seeks to reveal the theatrical frameworks which have perpetuated a static acceptance of a fictional performance. Butler calls the fabrication of gender "inevitable," but suggests that gender's fabrication must reveal the construction of masculinity and femininity, and corrupt the notion that these attributes have a sexed origin from which they are naturally produced. As with much of the work explored in this book, she suggests "playing," and "replaying" subversive possibilities.[22]

Butler lays out the restrictive frameworks of gender, sex, and sexuality, and the acts of imitation which ironically fortify those frameworks through the familiarity of the performance. If normative practices of gender and sexuality have been established through repeated performance, then I propose that queer and feminist gender performances offer the alternative identities and desires that reject those normative limitations.

Jennifer Blessing, curator of the Guggenheim exhibition *Rrose is Rrose is a Rose: Gender Performance in Photography*, echoes this. She approaches gender performance as its own mode of defense against the cyclic restriction considered by Butler. She identifies the subjects she included in the exhibition (the performers of gender) as being in control and void of self-doubt.[23] She frames performance as the source of this power.

I'm interested in how new performances can fuck up and expose old performances. Gender need not reenact meanings that are socially established, nor can representations of sexuality and desire reflect the same stasis. Queerness responds to the perpetuation of heterosexuality as the standard that Butler maintains is at the root of our most detrimental gender norms. Jodie Taylor, author of *Playing it Queer: Popular Music, Identity, and Queer World Making*, qualifies queerness as "resistance imbued with anti-assimilationist and de-constructionist rhetoric that aggressively opposes hegemonic identificatory and behavioural norms, including liberal lesbian and gay identity politics."[24] This summarizes a theoretical intention of queerness, with which I agree — a sort of constructive dissonance — though she maintains that queerness can take many tangible and intangible forms: "a political or ethical approach, an aesthetic quality, a mode of interpretation or way of seeing, a perspective or orientation, or a way of desiring, identifying or dis-identifying."[25] From her list, I'm particularly concerned with the power of queer aesthetics. In *Cruising Utopia: The Then and There of Queer Futurity*, José Muñoz says that, "Often we can glimpse the worlds proposed and promised by queerness in the realm of the aesthetic. The aesthetic, especially the queer aesthetic, frequently contains blueprints and schemata of a forward-dawning futurity."[26] Muñoz's attention to the future derives from his claim that "Queerness is not yet here."[27] He envisions a queerness necessarily, permanently, on a horizon toward which we must continue to advance. However, the scope of this book is such that queer aesthetics explored in seminal works *do* forecast the even more saturated queer worlds explored in contemporary media. The queer aesthetics we will explore resist the common framework of gender, but also offer and affirm the queer possibility proposed by Muñoz.

Other feminist and queer literature which has been most crucial to this book focuses less on the historic subordination of women and the queer community, than on cultivating agency through sexual provocation and self-possession, and disrupting hetero-sexist paradigms through queer sexual representation. There's a classic quote in *Right-Wing Women*, where radical, anti-pornography feminist Andrea Dworkin says, "No woman needs intercourse; few can escape it."[28] Dworkin describes sex as an oppressive practice. She only considers sex in a heterosexual context. Let's compare this to the sentiments of Paul B. Preciado in *Testo Junkie: Sex, Drugs, and Biopolitics*. Preciado draws from feminist music critic Ellen Willis, summarizing that feminists who seek to abolish pornography, and other forms of female sexual representation make themselves complicit to the patriarchal structures in a heterosexual society that represses and controls women's bodies.[29] Rather than participating in this historical policing of female bodies and sexuality, I support the expression of a sexuality whose explicitness is interpreted as defiant, rather than complicit.

Though in this instance Preciado's point, like Dworkin's text, derives from a heterosexual, cisgender model, *Testo Junkie* also functions in a queer feminist capacity. In the text Preciado documents their illegal consumption of testosterone as a sexed female before transitioning. They describe filmed performances of drag and masturbation. What is described is a queer sexuality: forms of pleasure, desire, and performance that combat heteronormative models organized according to heterosexual male desire. In this book, I operate from a pro-sex feminist view, according to a reevaluation of the agency available in sexual representation, and further highlight the importance of queer sexual representation to destabilizing the heterosexist frameworks which inform Dworkin's thinking.

This book explores both the erotic sexual representations explored by Preciado, and representations of sex which unhinge gendered aesthetics from the sex historically perceived as their origin. Use of various forms of sexual representation, however, is not the only means of creating queer and feminist work. Jack Halberstam, N. Katherine Hayles, and Donna Haraway have all approached feminism via a notion of the posthuman, which also proposes an alternative to the binary model of gender.

In her book *Simians, Cyborgs, and Women: The Reinvention of Nature* Haraway positions her feminist perspective in relation to the figure of the cyborg. She thinks that, in causal terms, if we can make robots we should be able to re-make ourselves. The implications are big. She wants a whole new social reality. She wants liberation, consciousness, the end of oppression.[30] She calls the cyborg, "a creature in a post-gender world."[31] She suggests that our proven ability to construct the future can be geared toward the production of alternative gender possibilities. As a non-human creation, the cyborg subverts sex and destabilizes sexual norms.

However, Haraway also uses the cyborg to approach feminism in a way that questions the movement's capacity to unify. Because the cyborg calls taxonomic categorization into question (no more men, no more women (only Zuul)), Haraway calls for unity based on, "affinity, conscious coalition, and political kinship,"[32] rather than identity. This book will try to reinforce this project by including a scope of subjectivities whose identification as queer and feminist is signified by a shared resistance to further marginalization. But that said, the intersectional approaches of some authors have also served to provide more nuanced interpretations of various objects of study.

Examples of such authors include Mae Gwendolyn Henderson, who explains in the introduction to *Queer Black Studies: A Critical Anthology* that:

> [...] as some theorists have noted, the deconstruction of binaries and the explicit "unmarking" of difference (e.g., gender, race, class, region, able-bodiedness, etc.) has serious implications for those for whom these other differences "matter" [...] To ignore the multiple subjectivities of the minoritarian subject within and without political movements and theoretical paradigms is not only politically and theoretically naive, but also potentially dangerous.[33]

This passage highlights that, although queer and feminist projects can be constructed around the inclusionary approach explored by Haraway, this does not preclude attending to, or making visible, the differences among subjects and their lived experiences within those projects.

Gender performance can establish new meanings of gender through subversive acts. And though this text focuses on some particularly theatrical and commercial performances of gender, I'd like to clarify that their subversive power does not rely on documentation or audience. Compelling visual strategies are worthy of close analysis, but gender subversion is not uniquely anchored to any medium or context.

X.

The strings held two short strands of dark green glass beads, one lying above the other, drawn into silver clasps, and exited to be strung as a single strand. The silver clasp on the left was in the shape of a leaf, adorned at its edges with emerald gemstones. In the middle, to accentuate the points of the leaf, were three pearls, one at each point. The clasp on the right was O-shaped. There were dark green gemstones on it as well.

The image of me wearing this necklace, of the space from above my breasts, my shoulders, my mouth, with a sheen of perspiration from July's heat, is the earliest one I have found that was sent to him after I moved to New York. What began with panic attacks and feelings of self-pity plummeted, as if from the edge of a cliff, at a terminal velocity into a morbid abyss, a hell, a cold, an erasure, a paralysis. This depression had physical symptoms. I had gotten used to the hyperventilation. I had lived through each episode without collapse or loss of consciousness, which would have suggested to me that I needed to tell someone, which was my real concern when they began. Tears would come without any trigger at all, my throat would close, and my left arm would seize and left hand clench. The attacks frustrated me, and even the tiniest bit of resistance intensified them disproportionately. I treated this malfunction of chemistry with therapy and prescribed drugs, but also wrongfully used sex with, and performances for, this man to self-medicate. At the time I did think I was in love with him. Deconstructed, it was the being seen and being fucked by him that temporarily lifted the feeling of death, which was invisibility. Like a drug, I selfishly consumed him to relieve pain, or to feel anything. Relapse was cyclical, exhausting, pathetic, and from a purely aesthetic standpoint, gorgeous.

He came over and pulled that necklace off my throat. He pulled gently until one strand broke, then the other, and was able to drag the beads down the front of my body. One of the strands left intact I wrapped around his dick when I blew him, and let press into my labia when we fucked.

We returned to a collaborative dynamic that obscured the lines of what was real and performed. Like the necklace there was always an object around which we worked, or, as we had become accustomed to in the early phases of our courtship, a place we chose to be that framed and intensified us.

Ribbons: I had several yards of long black satin ribbon, from which I would cut smaller swatches to tie into my hair — long languid ones, nothing too sweet or bow-like. As I had done for him in the images I sent years earlier, he would wrap me up in this ribbon until it produced its own tangled knots. When he would lay on top of me, nearly motionless, letting me open and soften, he would pull, gently, from anywhere, and the subtle restriction around my neck, or between my fingers, or that wrapped around the inside of my thigh, would make me pour for him. Everything was impossibly slow. Intentionally, impossibly slow. He would reach his hand into my hair, pull it back until my jaw dropped and lick the roof of my mouth. He pressed his teeth against mine until I thought they would break.

Whiskey: Objects might be dictated by obvious changes around us. When it got cold we fetishized whiskey and dark bars, and fucking drunk. What started with warming glasses of whiskey neat at the candlelit Bowery Hotel bar disintegrated at home, pressed against the wall, passing burning mouthfuls of Jameson between our lips, letting it run down our necks and soak into our clothes. As we drank we clawed and bit, and laughed our fucking heads off. I grabbed his face with both hands and inhaled his tongue. We didn't stop until the bottle was empty.

The intensity of these encounters was predicated on an established history, but I didn't see him often. He had been busy with work and vague about the status of any relationship. To be clear, it had become painful again when he went silent. I was still just too proud to demand some sort of consistency, or even definition in our relationship. I hadn't heard from him in over two weeks when he suggested that we have drinks at the Bowery. It was a cool night, but we were sat outside under the heating lamps on the red garden chairs that overlook a small old cemetery trapped between buildings on Second Ave. I confessed that I thought we'd still end up together because we were the only ones terrible enough for each other. I was referring to our shared culpabilities in the affair previously, and the torrid nature of our physical connection. He said that wasn't going to happen, which did not phase me. It felt more like he was dismissing the idea of us being terrible, and had just delivered the wrong organization of words to form his rebuttal. I began on another unrelated point. He interrupted me gently, but physically, by placing his hand on my thigh, and said again, slowly, that it was not going to happen. He was telling me something else, but I was not ready to know it yet. And when I did know it, I could not speak it. My eyes flooded but my years of denying Aaron the satisfaction of verifying his wounds with my tears had prepared me well for a moment such as this. A scene wasn't going to be of any use at this point. There was a bit more calm, but brief discussion, and eventually we got the bill, paid, exited, he kissed me on the cheek, and we moved in opposite directions. I turned around and called to him, because in a movie the better girl would. I could do it, and deliver it with earnest, because I knew it was right, even if it was not sourced from a genuine emotion: Ian... congratulations.

X.

I released the songs I made with Mark as my first solo EP that summer, and in the winter started working with a producer, Ryan Kelly, who I was introduced to by way of mutual friends from Seattle. Ryan was familiar with the band and completely on board. I went into overdrive, trying to shake the grief for our band and my lover that had turned into a gray existence. I went to classes from 8:30am–3:30pm, worked at the hotel 4:00pm–12:30am, and would then often meet Ryan at the studio where he was a staff engineer after his sessions ended, from 1–3am, to record our stuff. I also interned at a gallery on weekends. I never called in sick and I never took drugs to make me go faster.

Ryan then introduced me to a keyboard player and writing partner, Ashley Jurgemeyer, based in Los Angeles. We holed up together in her apartment in LA, and wrote most of the record in a week. Like me, she had been in aggressive bands with men for most of her adolescence and early adulthood. She had been in relationships with collaborators, and other musicians, and expressed the traumas of being treated as disposable. Like Mark, Ryan and Ashley highlighted the dysfunction of previous collaborations, and that they were not unique to my experience. I still felt mostly blank despite knowing what I wanted and taking steps to get it. Confrontational female pop stars were proliferating around me, and I wanted to be among them.

X.

Lady Gaga's *Alejandro* video was directed by fashion photographer Steven Klein, who has said that the video explores, "The pain of living without your true love."[34] This theme is dramatized through the narrative of death and desire. Lady Gaga leads the funeral procession of her dead lover, then becomes a nun, signifying her commitment to a life of celibacy in their absence. Images of fire and violence run throughout the video, reinforcing the sense of profound loss through their suggestion of destruction. Lady Gaga represents herself as sexually unavailable, but includes a plethora of queer male icons, who seem to serve as the prostheses for her sexuality. Her homoerotic fantasies allow her to dramatize her desire outside a heteronormative framework. The individual figures also seem to express specific meanings, which further confuse historical boundaries of gender identity and sexuality.

The first shot of the video pans away from a man in a leather, police-style, biker cap, who sleeps slumped in a chair with his legs crossed, wearing fishnet tights and black stiletto heels. His chest is bare. In front of him is an AK-47 rifle and an ashtray full of cigarettes [Figure 1].

Figure 1: Lady Gaga, *Alejandro*, 2010

As the camera pulls away we see him in the company of several other men dressed in a similar sexual, biker uniform. There are several attacks on gender in just this opening shot. The characters in the video are modeled after police officers or other militant figures. Rather than being at attention, expressing authority, responsibility, and control, they rest, even sleep, with their bodies languidly draped amongst club chairs, denouncing the expectations of their masculinity. The expected attitude of these gendered subjects has been corrupted by their poses, despite their being equipped with weapons. Their fishnets and heels marry a sexy and feminine drag aesthetic to that of the queer "daddy," "leatherman," and "clone" stereotypes. While the characters are portrayed as lazy and unthreatening, it is implied that violence may be imminent. These characters simultaneously subvert classic hetero-male masculinity, while lending potentially violent authority to both the feminine drag character and the queer stereotypes.

The next sequence shows a different group of similarly

militant-looking men in a fashionable, minimalist uniform. The characters arguably seem to reference the aesthetic of popular New York DJs, the Misshapes, who have been closely aligned with queer nightlife and high fashion [Figure 2]. They wear black shorts and boots, with their hair either cropped into a precision Vidal Sassoon-style bowl cut or covered by ominous masks.

Figure 2: The Misshapes, 2008

The group marches down a ramp, eventually dispersing into the darkness, as the first shot of Lady Gaga is revealed. Her lips are an intense red, though the rest of her face is obscured by an elaborate, bionic-looking headdress. The thick, glass lenses of the seemingly masculine, industrial-looking apparatus are covered by a feminine, black lace. Lady Gaga is shown leading a funeral procession dressed in a couture variation of a widow's ensemble [Figure 3]. The male characters' hypersexual representations are offset by suggestions that she may be asexual — either because she is in mourning or part machine. She reinforces this by later costuming herself in a nun's habit made of oxblood

PVC material. She lays in a bed of black satin sheets and pillows, surrounded by a pile of jeweled rosaries. Around the time of the video's production, she had claimed to be celibate — that her career was preventing her from meeting people.[35] This suggests that Lady Gaga represents her own sexuality through the nun character. She controls the male figures, drawing on them to express the erotic masculine desire that presently eludes her.

Figure 3: Lady Gaga, *Alejandro*, 2010

Gaga's control is reinforced by another homoerotic idol shown sitting on a bed surrounded by puppet-like strings, which perhaps she operates. He holds a gold gun as a kind of phallic symbol of his masculinity and virility. In the dance sequences that follow, she observes from a detached position of authority above.

The camera moves to full shots of the dancers, who perform in front of a projection of raging flames. Their movements are intensely masculine and sexual: they flex their muscles, throw themselves to the concrete floor, thrust their pelvises into the air with arched backs, and gather in a circular huddle. The men ultimately separate into pairs, where the homoerotic themes become more explicit and the dance moves more intimately aggressive. Choreography transgresses into physical entanglements reminiscent of sport wrestling. One couple engages in a stylized choking scene where one partner grabs the other's neck before rolling his body back, diffusing the violence through the erotic motion. Still in pairs, one of the partners grabs the other by the waist and throws them in a plank position to the concrete floor while mounted above him [Figure 4]. The masculinity of wrestling and sports huddles has been appropriated into a highly choreographed homoerotic display, subverting the hetero-sexist paradigms of fraternity and violence.

Figure 4: Lady Gaga, *Alejandro*, directed by Steven Klein, (2010)

In the next montage, Lady Gaga engages with the dancers, theatricalizing a sexual exchange of dominant roles. She straddles a man in heels who lays face down on a bed, then simulates sex beneath one of her male counterparts. She is picked up from behind with her legs wrapped around the man's body, while he places his hand around her throat. In this sequence, the position of dominance and masculinity is repeatedly exchanged in a kind of choreographed battle, perhaps bringing us to question how these factors impact our desire for the subject that displays them.

After the funeral procession, Lady Gaga appears in a bra with a gun attached to each breast. Usually associated with sustaining life, her breast becomes a threatening weapon. Neither her body, nor her sexuality is available, but protected and fortified. The video returns to the group of young male dancers who throw Lady Gaga's body amongst them, while violently groping and kissing her. Images of fire, riots, and war continue to be intercut in a montage mirroring the provocative sexual images. These shots are then spliced with images of Lady Gaga in her nun costume, lying in bed, suggesting these are images she has fantasized. Widowed, she manifests her desire into a homoerotic fantasy that will not be consummated, protecting her vow of celibacy. The video concludes with Lady Gaga in bed in her oxblood nun's habit as her face disintegrates into burning circles of white light, conflating purity and destruction.

X.

In the video *Bad Girls*, M.I.A. uses her immediate critique of the Saudi Arabian laws that prohibited women from driving as a focal point to expose and confront broader sexisms and gender norms. She approaches this in two main ways: by re-stylizing traditional feminine dress and upending restrictive female norms through illegal and dangerous car stunts performed by women.

After sweeping shots of an empty desert, a tableau of Arab women is shown. They are fully covered, but wear dark sunglasses and silky layers with clashing, ostentatious prints: oversized cheetah spots, tiger stripes on gold, red paisley with swirling linked chains. Rejecting objectification of the gaze, they look directly into the camera, standing next to a silver BMW. Some slouch against the car, staring down the viewer. A woman at the front crosses her arms with head tilted threateningly down [Figure 5]. Their authoritative, unfazed air is shared by M.I.A., shown in the desert with hands on hips, as a fire burns in the distance, billowing smoke.

The shot changes to the interior of the car, where a woman grips and releases the wheel with her arm outstretched over the top of it as a physical cue for authority and anticipation. The slowed footage gives the scene

Figure 5: M.I.A., *Bad Girls*, (2012)

an entirely self-serving sensuality, compounded by the woman's turn away from the camera. She wears black leather gloves, with metallic, brooch-like embellishments up the length of her wrist that catch the light, and full makeup, with a heavily pencilled, angular brow, thick eyeliner, and dark lips. These extreme feminine aesthetics read as a practice of adornment, whose subversion is established through their placement within historically prohibited male spaces. In *Women Driving: Fiction and Automobile Culture in Twentieth Century America*, Deborah Clarke says that, "in providing access to the public sphere — to work, to escape — the car transformed women's lives as profoundly as suffrage."[36] She speaks about American culture, but describes the sense of freedom and choice that the subjects in M.I.A.'s video seek to access with the illegal stunts that follow.

By performing various car stunts, the female figures in *Bad Girls* not only defy the sexist, ideological authority that would reserve driving rights for men, but express further agency over their own bodies by placing them in vulnerable, dangerous physical situations. Two women lean out from each window of a moving car. The driver watches the road with her head out the window, her fist raised and clenched in the air in a gesture of empowerment. A mix of sped up and slowed down clips creates a jarring, anxious montage where cars spin out on the edges of their tires or race in a team at full speed. Exhaust billows, and the sound of screeching breaks is left in to cut through the track.

The crew of drivers, cars, and spectators grows, creating an entourage that feels like something between a gang and a parade. Two cars roll down the road on just their two side wheels, with a woman standing atop the leading car with arms outstretched. M.I.A. is shown perched on the side of another tilted vehicle, filing her nails nonchalantly in a nod to her femininity. As the scene turns to night, the women move into another dance scene in metallic and Day-Glo jumpsuits. The group of drivers and spectators move as a collective, led by M.I.A., with more stunts and images of the audience cheering them on. Subsequently, the driver of the car that M.I.A. was riding on leans their arm out their window and drags a knife along the road.

M.I.A. makes a direct attack on the particular driving restriction on women in Saudi Arabia at the time of filming, though the video's collapse of extreme feminine aesthetics with anti-authoritarian themes has a broader subversive reach. She uses a specific cultural context from which to position an appropriation of the historically male-aligned obsession with muscle cars' danger, speed, and power.

X

Brooke Candy's *Opulence* video begins with her attacking a man in a bathroom. Their quarrel over money leaves the man dead. Candy has twisted his neck between her stiletto heels. Though the Theater of Cruelty does not rely on the display of literal cruelty, it also does not exclude violence as a means of achieving its aims. In order to restore to the theater a passionate and convulsive conception of life, Artaud says that his theatrical cruelty will be bloody when necessary, but not systematically so.[37] This is perhaps the same credo Candy's character holds in relation to her survival. This opening act of literal violence can be seen as both a subversion of classic standards of femininity and exemplary of the kind of jarring action aligned with the Theater of Cruelty.

The next shot shows Candy behind a transparent bathroom cabinet, showing its contents and acting as a mirror for her. On the shelf of the cabinet is a glass cross standing upright, bottles of perfume, and a filled wine glass. In these shots, femininity is treated as having its own kind of artillery, used to weaponize the cisgender female body.

Candy is shown in various shots playing with feminine constructions of her identity. One shot shows her in a mask of diamonds, crafted to look like a skull, with wide, sunken eye-holes, and a broad, vacant mouth region. In another shot, she wears white contacts with oval pupils and has a line of rhinestones running down her face, with her lips covered in glitter [Figure 6].

Figure 6: Brooke Candy, *Opulence*, 2014

Over the course of the video, Candy assumes seven additional costumes. All are glamorous and complicated; layers of rhinestones, facemasks, and wigs or headdresses. Candy suggests that identity is not only unfixed, but potentially even disposable. Gender representation is subsumed by an array of full-body veneers.

We see Candy arrive at a party where the attendants are dressed in bondage and fetish gear, including a pair of French maids with nipple pasties and latex uniforms, who are later shown kissing. Candy lays down on a table at the party, where she spreads her legs and touches herself in front of the camera. Candy expresses agency and self-possession through explicit public view of her sexuality. She is both publicly on view as the center of the party and on view for the video's audience. She confronts the gaze of the camera, reminding us that despite this view, her body and self are ultimately unavailable to us. Candy echoes this power of withholding sex in an interview where she claims, "Pussy is a weapon [...] Women are so fucking powerful. Pussy is where life comes from [...] If we withheld sex, women would have all the power and that is why it is a weapon."[38]

Candy expresses the power of sexuality: its necessity for procreation and the power of women to control it. Germaine Greer echoes the power of the authoritative and possessive stance Candy takes, claiming that rather than sex being inherently oppressive to women, it is the historical insistence that women adopt a passive sexual role that must be dismantled.[39] As shown by her aggressive quotes and overt displays of sexuality, Candy is anything but passive.

The video concludes in a rapid succession of images of Candy, followed by her logo at the end of the video: two hands linked by a loose chain, presenting middle fingers, which are crossed over one another, underscored by the words, "FAG MOB," the name of Candy's creative team. It is of note that Fag Mob is here inclusive of the director, Steven Klein, who also directed Lady Gaga's *Alejandro* video, and Lady Gaga's former stylist, Nichola Formichetti. The relationship between the reoccurring themes of gender, and the creative pair stands to question the extent of Lady Gaga's or Brooke Candy's responsibility for crafting the subversive images with which they are so closely aligned. Throughout the video, gender is all but obscured, as the song suggests, through the opulence of costume. What remains is an aggressive sexual agency, put forth in a public space as self-possessed confrontation.

X.

I told him I was his girl. I pulled him aside and said I knew I didn't look like it in my hotel unfiorm, but I was. I could prove it. All I needed was his email. Just give me your email, I said. Trust me.

I was asked to print out their concert tickets at the hotel desk. His friend hung an arm around him, swaying a bit, imposing playfully with his much larger body, and said, "See this guy right here?! This guy just got promoted to A&R at Epic Records! I'm takin' him out to celebrate!" The new hire was smiling with an appreciable humility, with his head tucked down toward his phone. I printed the tickets, set them on the desk, and held my fingertips on them. Extending out toward his space, he naturally followed my arm with his gaze back toward its base, then met my eyes. This is when I told him what I could make true if I said it like it already was. I am your girl. I had no inclination whatsoever that this was a wrong, or embarrassing, or ridiculous thing to do. It was the only thing to do. It *was* true.

I got his business card, embossed, proved, with the Epic label, and retreated to the back office to email him. I apologized to my co-workers, panicked and dismissive, abandoning the cool confidence that the previous two minutes might have indicated was sourced from a me-shaped glacier under my skin. I left them to the wolves. I couldn't give a fuck: I needed to use the fucking internet.

Within minutes I had put together a makeshift press kit full of images, references, a rollout plan, three of the demos I had been working on with Ryan Kelly, and promises — that I was the best performer EVER, that I would blow his MIND. I concluded: All I want is music. Fuck love, fuck money, fuck life. Let me play you some songs.

The man got back quickly. He was impressed, and wanted to meet. He had listened to every track and found the singles I had put out the previous summer. He had feedback and questions on all of them:

> I love your voice/sound, and your energy comes across vividly on the two records. ladies and gentlemen is cool-- seems like it would sound/feel incredible live? I really like marrying kind, you definitely have a very unique sound. As far as your image do you have any other pictures? I like tazers and blazers track, is that you screaming on buffalo? This track is really sultry, a bit bizarre at points but its interesting. French waltz is pretty creepy but would love to hear at a vampire's funeral, if vampires had funerals. Big black is one of my most favorite of all your music. I like laser eyes too — think it would be a strong record for licensing (tv or film).
>
> I'd definitely like to hear more about your story, your vision and where you are with your career/music, etc.
>
> Where are you from originally? Do you speak french fluently? do you have footage of you performing?

Todd went by his initials, "TG." Such is the music industry. He was a sweetheart and a hustler, and he wanted to prove himself in his promotion as much as I did in music in general. Because my schedule was insane he met me frequently during my lunch breaks at the hotel, which happened in the evening and were only thirty minutes long. I never ever wanted him to see me as anything other than God, so I'd have him let me know when he was close by, change into something completely outrageous, and meet him on the stoop at the apartments next door to the hotel. Lady Gaga was in full swing, so fashion-wise, all bets were off. I liked to change into full skirts and crop tops with a bit of sparkle or other minimal embellishments on them. On the occasion that I forgot my change of clothes, though, it had been perfectly appropriate to the moment to wrap myself in one of the hotel's flat sheets, bound by a couple of black satin hair ribbons that had been floating around my bag. Heavy, dark eye-makeup and crimson lips were always applied, and subsequently removed, before getting back into the white dress shirt, tie, and jeans that comprised my hotel uniform. TG got me on a showcase, and I flew my writing partner, Ashley, out to play with me. Again, I did what I was supposed to do. I relished in its ease. I had adapted my trademark chaos to pop, and still had it. I convinced him. He was excited, and got me more shows in New York and Philadelphia.

I rounded the edge of my second autumn in New York and was finishing a thesis on Helmut Newton for my degree. I wanted to deconstruct his approach and understand why I felt so compelled by the women in his work. I learned to read the feminism in his hyper-sexual images. In a Newton image, there is always a subtle play with props, or angles, or costume, that puts the woman in control. This deeply informed my visual work, and was, at that point, my deepest immersion in queer and feminist literature. I wanted to ensure that I could always explain the power and logic of the image.

Classes had ended, so I spent my newly-free daytime hours interning at Christie's auction house Monday to Wednesday and at David Zwirner Gallery Thursday and Friday. I was still working at the hotel in the evenings. On the weekend, I worked reception at Paul Kasmin's second, smaller gallery space on 28th Street. I was aware that even if I did "make it," commercial careers don't always last long. All of this was for plan-B, but I also valued my investment in the art world for what it returned in visual direction. The record was nearly there. Much of its sound had been dictated by TG. He wanted the rock single, the pop single, the ballad. I gave them to him. I was willing to simplify my music if it meant I could take greater liberties with the images. Madonna, Lady Gaga, M.I.A. (and soon Beyoncé) had all proved that this was the contract: the bigger the hit, the weirder it can look. L.A. Reid had moved from Island Def Jam to Epic Records, and TG wanted me to play for Reid when he returned after the holidays from being a judge on *The X Factor* in Los Angeles. It struck me that the band's history had come full circle, and I was going to be back in front of L.A. I couldn't wait. I was going to the gym, plotting out the launch of the album, the videos. I figured I would get one chance, and visualized that moment on repeat.

In the meantime, TG asked if I wanted to try writing for Avril Lavigne, who they were having a hard time re-branding. What? Ridiculous, but of course I did. This was another new level I hadn't prepared myself for by wanting it for years. To write for an established pop star — however outside my personal arena of taste — was an entirely unexpected gift and challenge.

Dudes — people like to write pop songs LATE. I did two sessions at Quad studios, where in 1994 Tupac Shakur had been shot five times in the lobby and survived. Both of these sessions started after midnight. The studio was in Times Square, and TURBO. There were blue neon tubes surrounding the ceiling perimeter of the lobby, a pool table, and bar area. It was a bottle of Hpnotiq manifested into a habitable interior. Again, I showed up dressing the part. I wore a white mini dress, unzipped down its back, so that the bodice could be completely folded over; its boning turned out against my leg. On top I wore a black lace bra and covered my neck with a fox fur. I wore gold sunglasses and leather driving gloves. I was paired with a producer who went by the name "Deputy." A Google search out of curiosity would later prove that despite the ridiculous moniker, he had gone on to turn out hits that double as personal faves, such as Rhianna's "Bitch Better Have My Money." Deputy had an overwhelming library of tracks. Scrolling through their titles, nicknames such as "Ideas for JT" and "Hov demo," did not end. He asked me what I wanted, but didn't know my references. I thought a mildly electronic version of the Breeders might be a comeback recipe for Avril. He was impatient and disinterested from the beginning, but not rude. He knew, but I did not, that he would put the track on a loop and leave the room until I was done writing to it. Every night he still had to be there to cruise his own library so some ding-dong could write while he waited. He would drink and play pool. I was left alone, and drank coffee from a Styrofoam cup and hoped that this would be my life. I could not silence the interior audio reminding me not to blow it. Two or so hours later we recorded my vocal and melody. Oddly, the strangers around the lobby invited themselves to this part of the session. They filled the leather couch in the room and nodded in approval without lifting their heads from their phones. The song was sent to TG, who said he liked it, but that it sounded too much like me. He sent me back. I had another stab, sent the new track and waited. I didn't hear anything. I had been texting him and the messages weren't going through. Same with emails. I felt like I could not do a single thing until I knew what was going on. Was it really that bad? Had this failed attempt at pop gold for Avril erased his excitement over the tracks of mine which had been tailor-made for him? I got a call from a number I didn't recognize and answered it. It was TG. I expressed my concern and asked if everything was ok. Was the song OK, was he OK, when was L.A. coming back to New York?

He apologized that I hadn't been able to get ahold of him. The label had disconnected his work phone when they laid him off two days before. He really liked the song.

X.

This is a common fate in the music industry. But that didn't change the way it felt.

X.

X.

TG was let go right before Christmas, which I was meant to spend with one of my best friends from high school and his wife. The bad news hadn't come with adequate time to get myself home to Seattle for some greater sense of safety, or at least physical distance from it. Flights were now prohibitively expensive. I was angry and impatient with strangers, but I displayed this in a blank, disassociated way. I gave single-word answers and responses could take several seconds. Every single thing, from brushing my teeth, to crossing the street, eating to sleeping, hurt, because none of it was the thing that had been taken away, in the same way, again.

I received two messages at the same time on Christmas morning. Because of the time difference my mother's would come later. One was from my friend, Gary, telling me that his wife, a dancer, Jessi, had thrown her back out, and they couldn't join me. They had to go to ER. The other was from Ian, wishing me Merry Christmas. I told Gary I totally understood, and sent love. I told Ian, *fuck you*, and went to see the new Tarantino movie alone. Regrettably, this was not actually a refusal of his return.

X.

He opened every part of me, and this was the only thing I could feel. When he came into me from behind, he seemed to pass gently though consecutive rings, each gripping around him with varying intensities until terminating at a soft bay that was wired to my spine. When he held me here I could feel him in my throat, and my stomach, my clitoris, and my eyes. To relax my neck, I laid down when he fucked my mouth. His shins either side of my trunk, knees nestled up toward my armpits, his body up and folded over me, nearly in a prayer position. He ran his dick along the edges of my teeth, over and over in a circular motion. For months, he came over and laid on me, and in me, and his guilt and my pain made for durational orgasms. Because when you lack the entitlement and the ambition for celebratory friction, for fucking, the most sensitive recesses of your interior unfold under sustained, motionless, pressure like a sea anemone. The images we used to operate around went away and we had nothing to speak about. I wasn't under any illusion that this meant anything, but I was grateful for some respite from despair, even if the replacement with sensation was also accompanied by shame.

X.

A few directionless months passed. It was spring. I didn't hear from him for a few days and turned to the internet. There wasn't much there. He didn't post much, but through .jpegs labelled by year I tried to manifest his presence and the honest reasons why he didn't want me right that second. I found his youngest brother's feed on Twitter. He was a musician. I was familiar with him from my time spent with his family in Pennsylvania. Maybe there could be a lead. At the top of the page there was an exchange between him and someone wanting to record. Ian's brother said he'd love to, but that he'd have to wait a bit because his brother's wife was due to give birth that week and he wanted to be there.

He said his brother's wife was due to give birth that week and he wanted to be there.

He said his brother's wife was due to give birth that week and he wanted to be there.

There are three brothers. The third brother is also married.

But.

Did you know that if you type your lover's name into that tiny Google box, followed by the word "baby," you may find his and his wife's baby registry? Surely I'm not the only one that has found this out the worst way.

X.

Whereas marriage is known to fail, and can be undone, children are irreversible. The child had been born the week that Ian absented himself from my bed without reason. He had nine months to tell me, and didn't. When I emailed to tell him I was done now and that he should have told me, he had the audacity to write back, "tell you what?" The obscene, genuine bluff was followed with the pledge to call in a half hour. I told him that he was not to call me then, or ever. If I got one call or text or email — it would be hideous. He left me alone. I said earlier that I would be sorry. I was, I am sorry. Consequences born of deplorable decisions do not warrant sympathy. This is a cautionary tale.

The mess coincided with my friend Sam's visit from Seattle. He had tickets to see Pulp's reunion show at Radio City Music Hall and took me. Pulp weren't big in America like they were in the UK. I only knew their single from the *Great Expectations* soundtrack. Watching them, I was filled with joy for the first time since TG sent me to the recording studio five months earlier. Jarvis scaled various platforms that flanked the stage. He wiggled and shimmied. He entertained. He soaked up our adoration and recycled it back into us. In that moment Pulp reminded me of the way back to myself — music, performance, dancing, sex.

That summer, I took on an internship at *Interview Magazine* that would turn into several years of freelance writing for them. For months, while updating the exhibition calendar or unassumingly making photocopies of the archive for my own pleasure, I only listened to Pulp. Their songs are great, but it was the performative aspect of this that was probably more gratifying — a durational work that signified an attention to the parts of my identity that I honored, but was not quite ready to re-engage with. Pulp could be my surrogate. I wore them like a cast. When taken to their conceptual extremes, performances with the lowest stakes can become remarkable. If the gravity isn't there, this can still produce humor. I took this performance to the nth degree because I could and because I thought it was funny: I decided to move to London to study at an arts college like the girl in "Common People" that Jarvis thinks is so alluring. I know the song is based on its criticality of her character, but it was a way of romanticizing an exit from New York that was fundamentally necessary.

On my last night in New York, I went with Nabil to the Roseland Ballroom to see Ian Astbury perform his Cult album, *Electric*. This had been a record on heavy rotation during overnight drives on tour. It was nostalgic, but it was also an attempt to mark my departure in some relatively fun way in hopes of making it memorable.

Nabil and I separated after the show to use the bathrooms and met back up outside. He said that he had just received an email from the wine shop across from his office announcing a secret Prince show that would take place that night. I wasn't sure why Prince was playing a wine shop, but I told Nabil to please buy the tickets, and even if they were $500, do it, I would pay him back. We took a cab to Tribeca from 52nd Street, which you wouldn't normally do if you lived in New York. We arrived to find a queue of people around the block, with the following notice posted to the building:

Purple Rules
***No PHOTOGRAPHY
***No VIDEO recording
***No Cell Phones
These rules will be strictly enforced and
Violators will be asked to access another experience

It was happening. The venue was City Winery, a large chain wine shop with a small stage that Nabil said typically hosted acoustic sets for tastings and other small events. Prince came on at 1:30am. In front of him there was a speaker, in front of that there was a man, and behind him was me. His set included a mix of New Power Generation songs and songs with his new project at the time, a band comprised of him and three women, 3RDEYEGIRL. When he heard something he liked, he scrunched his face up like he'd just smelled a foot. My chemistry felt re-set. I had arrived at the oracle, and could be transported safely into my next life, a new dimension (I mean, I think this is how the person that would make you "access another experience" for having used a camera phone would put it).

The show let out about 3am, and I walked home slowly through Soho and the Lower East Side. There was a blue glow from the street lamps, and I looked up at the fire escapes and industrial windows that I loved. The sun started coming up in the last few blocks of my walk. I had given up my apartment a week before my departure and was staying with a friend for a few days, Lapshan. Before I left for the Cult show he told me that the woman he had been seeing, that he was certain he was in love with, had broken things off. I arrived home to find that he had painted a full-sized splitting axe black. He had leant it against the cupboards below the sink to dry. Love can justify anything.

X.

As in *Erotica*, Nine Inch Nails' (NIN) video, *Happiness in Slavery* incorporates similar dark, sexual imagery based on power dynamics and the inter-play of pleasure and pain. In the work of NIN, however, the focus is on pain *as* the sexual experience rather than part of it — part of the kissing, touching, dancing, and scenes in bed that are included in Madonna's work. It should be noted that the title of NIN's song is taken from a chapter of the classic erotic novel published under the pseudonym Pauline Réage, *The Story of O*; about a woman who commits herself to a submissive sexual lifestyle, only to realize her control in being the object of her lovers' desire and devotion. Also of note is the video's star, Bob Flanagan, a performance artist known for his masochistic work, which he felt mirrored the pain caused by his struggle with cystic fibrosis.

The video begins with the lead singer, Trent Reznor, in a cell. Black-and-white floral imagery precedes onanistic industrial gears grinding and pumping, creating a subversive juxtaposition of natural and mechanical symbols of fertility and production. We see Flanagan's character enter a deteriorated, windowless room in a suit. In the center of the room is an antique medical examination table — an indication that the character is somehow "sick." Flanagan places a dark rose at an altar where he lights a candle, then removes his clothes. As if purifying himself, he washes his body before a mirror, where his image recedes into the distance, ultimately disappearing, foreshadowing his death. Extremely rare is the exposure of Flanagan's full-frontal nudity, which, in addition to the video's extreme violence, contributed to the video being banned by MTV upon its release.

Flanagan lies down on the table, which suddenly turns mechanical. His body is tilted upright, and he is locked in at his wrists. A close-up shot of his hand shows metal carpenter's nails slowly driving into his flesh. Flanagan's face cringes, communicating the ecstatic pain, which he has knowingly committed himself to. A metal claw is positioned over Flanagan, gripping parts of his chest. Another metal grip pulls at his testicles. The claw makes another motion, diving into his chest, drawing blood, and pulling away part of his flesh. Blood drips into the pile of dead flowers around the table. Worms flash before the screen alluding to Flanagan's death and burial. The machine's attack continues until we are shown an overhead shot of Flanagan's splayed body. The metal sides of the machine fold over the corpse. The body is then presumably ground within the makeshift coffin before the remnants exit the machine, again into the pile of worms and flowers. Reznor is shown entering the room and beginning the same ritual placement of the rose and candle completed by Flanagan, suggesting that the cycle will begin again.

The aesthetics employed by NIN are grotesque, shocking, and subversively interlaced with masochistic eroticism. Authors who have explored and reinforced Artaud's cruelty in other mediums, but through similar lenses, are noteworthy here: these include Maggie Nelson's *The Art of Cruelty* and Kathy O'Dell's *Contract with the Skin*. Nelson uses Artaud's manifesto, "The Theater of Cruelty," as her lens. She identifies work of a literally violent nature, exemplifying Artaud's attention to shaking his audience. In a discussion of Francis Bacon, Nelson makes a point about Artaudian works:

> Welcome to Bacon's bracing allure (which resembles that of Artaud, and of Nietzsche) which posits this "violent return to life" as a way to restore us, or deliver us anew, to an un-alienated, unmediated flow of existence characterized by a more authentic relation to the so-called real. Unlike so many avant-gardists and revolutionaries, however, Bacon does not think or hope that this restored vitality will bring about the subsequent waning of inequalities, injustices or radical forms of suffering.[40]

What Nelson explains is that the reality exposed by these works of art may not necessarily be an easier one in which to exist. Bringing awareness to "inequalities, injustices, and suffering" does not make them less problematic, but rather — through their visibility and acknowledgement — more present than before. In the following passage, the same issue of unveiling reality is taken up by O'Dell, whose book explores masochism in the performance work of Chris Burden, Vito Acconci, and the collaborations of Marina Abramovic and Ulay:

Masochism blows the whistle on institutional frameworks that trigger it and within which it is practiced. Given the historical contexts of these performances, then, artists such as Burden seemed to be urging their viewers to pay attention to these facts: battles cannot be waged without sadists and masochists; soldiers at war in Vietnam are merely sadists and masochists by other names and the military is an institution established to train, sanction, and glorify sadists and masochists.[41]

This passage echoes Nelson's by asserting that masochistic art only lifts the veil on masochism within our culture and its institutions. In this regard, these works are unified not in solving a problem, but in exposing it through a coded visual vernacular. I suggest that Nine Inch Nails and Bob Flanagan also speak through this vernacular. On the surface, they expose subversive, sexual acts of masochism into the mainstream, but also make the pointed attempt at signifying the "institutional framework" which pathologizes and condemns sex.

Similar artistic tactics were used by playwright and performance theorist Friedrich Dürrenmatt, who is known for the term "Theater of the Grotesque." One of the major tenets of his work was "paradox," which we see mirrored in the pairing of pleasure and pain in *Happiness in Slavery*. Dürrenmatt elaborates on his idea of paradox, saying that our world has led us to the grotesque just as to the atomic bomb; that the grotesque is the only ostensible expression of dark, formless things.[42]

For Dürrenmatt, and I argue for NIN, performance of the grotesque gives shape and symbol to intangible destruction and horror. Dürrenmatt notes the creative property of art as paradoxical to this particular task, though comparing it to of our creation of the atomic bomb, which is antithetical to our very existence. In this capacity the grotesque images in *Happiness in Slavery* capture and mirror an already abject world, but in some way stall, or perhaps even reverse, that abjection through what are ultimately still generative creative acts.

X.

I am telling you all this to give it shape. This is not an absolution. It undoes nothing. How I chose to justify this love was to adapt and extend what I once shared with only one person. In this way, it is no longer just his. It is no longer for him.

I went to England and completed a practice-based PhD in the Visual Cultures Department at Goldsmiths, University of London. I appropriated the visual practice that had been cultivated as a way of communicating love and desire. The videos I continued to make were used as music videos or as projections during live shows. I still perform. My thesis located queer and feminist agency in music videos' sexually subversive performances. It responded to the subjugation of women and questioned heteronormative practices and binaries. Through a broader social interrogation, I admit, I tried to reconcile aspects of my history of making music and videos with people I loved. What follows is an edited version of that text, whose inclusion began earlier in this book. In lieu of a more classical academic introduction, I have marked the development of my interests and concerns as they arose alongside sex, subversion, and music video.

PART TWO

X.

Radical sexual representation is at the core of music video's historical controversies and its contemporary visual economy. MTV banned Madonna's video *Erotica* for its nudity and graphic BDSM scenes. Mykki Blanco explored queer and virtual sex in *Loner*, which was co-produced by PornHub. And, in her *Formation* video, Beyoncé confronts the camera with both of her middle fingers raised. Her manicured nails are painted a deep red; she wears diamonds and a black couture gown, and sings about getting "fucked good." In these works, performance is utilized to attack social norms and limitations of gender. The performance of gender itself is exposed through actions which are dissonant to a rubric of expected behaviors, historically considered natural.

A close visual analysis of the medium's erotic and confrontational iconography exposes how categories of sex and gender have been subverted through queer and feminist performances in music video since the launch of MTV in 1981. It was at this point that music video entered domestic space and became a fixture of the music industry. Music videos have since maintained their cultural ubiquity and produced perpetually experimental, lurid, and provocative sexual imagery.

X.

The ways in which the technological developments of the early 2000s changed music video's modes of production, distribution, consumption, and regulation are all inextricably linked to the proliferation of subversive gender representations in the medium. Perhaps most significant among these developments was the launch of YouTube, in 2005. Through the addition of advertisements played before a viewer's selected content, YouTube allowed the music industry to monetize the medium online and recoup some of the losses on music sales caused by illegal downloading of music through websites such as Napster and Pirate Bay that emerged in the late 1990s and early 2000s. The budgets for music videos had been severely reduced because of this in turn. Several record companies also banded together to create a similar website, Vevo,[1] where directors could incorporate product placement for additional revenue.[2] Whereas music videos were previously used as advertisements for the sale of the song for which they were made, they now had their own monetary potential. Garnering online traffic justified a renewed investment in the visual economy of an artist.

With this growth of an online viewing platform, it became less crucial to adhere to the regulations imposed by television stations such as MTV. While the banning of Madonna's *Justify My Love* video for its explicit sexual content has become somewhat legendary — a sufficient promotional tool in itself — few artists could have sacrificed the support of MTV in a similar way to that of Madonna, before YouTube. In an industry where MTV visibility was intensely competitive for its promotional value, incorporating sexually provocative material could be too great a risk.[3]

For independent artists and directors, the site provided a place to distribute music and video, which legitimized the DIY production of media that could suddenly be accessed as easily as work by mainstream artists. It made a popular and open forum available to queer artists and queer representation that had been historically marginalized by commercial industries. Change in regulations has triggered the production of more provocative content, while YouTube's open platform for distribution and consumption has proved integral to allowing amateur musicians and directors to produce, consume, and distribute queer work.

The technological factors which saw returned revenue to music video and greater license to visual content occurred in conjunction with dramatic social change, which may also have informed the queer and feminist content of contemporary video work. In 2015, same-sex marriage was legalized throughout the United States after the Supreme Court ruled state-level bans to be unconstitutional. Same-sex marriage has been legal in the United Kingdom since 2013. Since the first legalization of same-sex marriage in an American state in 2003, the extremity and prevalence of subversive representations of gender has increased in both commercial music videos and in those by artists outside the mainstream. While it is not my intention to establish a direct causality between same-sex marriage rights and music video, the parallel progression poses relevant questions of cultural assimilation. Has queer culture penetrated popular culture as a byproduct of greater gender and sexual equality that we might see as confirmed by same-sex marriage rights? Is it a more tenuous relationship of hetero-sexist commercial culture co-opting the queer market through its representation, while reinforcing the illusion of superiority by acting as gatekeepers to other social structures and ceremonies, such as marriage? Or, is music video a platform for anti-assimilation — a place where queer representations combat heteronormative conformity? Similar questions about which audience these images ultimately serve come up with regard to the hyper-sexual depiction of women in music video: are they feeding a patriarchal desire for objectified bodies and skin, or reinforcing their sexual agency in third-wave feminist defiance? These questions will be explored alongside analysis of the videos, which ultimately exemplify a growing consciousness of gender rights and roles, evidenced by a period whose radicalism can be measured in definitive political change.

These conditions accommodated the "radical proliferation of gender" that Butler called for to displace gender norms. This section seeks to establish the landscape of contemporary music video as a vital site where this radical proliferation and displacement occurs in ways that are unique to the medium and on an unparalleled scale. What other media deploys such a compelling lexicon of queer and feminist representation with the same level of visibility? How is this achieved? In the examples that follow, a myriad of genders and sexual identities are realized through a theatricalization of feminism and queerness that relies on an Artaudian approach. Social norms and limits are displaced in aggressive and fantastic ways via the agency of performance, implicating the theatricality of the most basic gender roles and the instability of gender categories outside the context of music video. To explore these claims, I'll examine individual works, and trends among artists' representations, which establish gender identities outside the historical binary.

The works considered below have been organized into a rough categorical index of queer and feminist representations. Though Butler encourages the proliferation of gender identities, it should be acknowledged that this particular method of research contradicts her opposition to "categories." She says that, "identity categories tend to be instruments of regulatory regimes, whether as the normalizing categories of oppressive structures or as the rallying points for a liberatory contestation of that very oppression."[4] Here, Butler illuminates the restrictive capacity of categories to be oppressive or co-opted toward a political agenda. She later clarifies, however, that a category may be acceptable, but that she prefers that it be "permanently unclear what it signifies."[5] Though this section explores gendered aesthetics under categorical headings, the intention is neither prescriptive, nor finite. This aesthetic inventory seeks less to populate new categorical meanings than to make the signification of the historical binary more "permanently unclear."

X. QUEER FEMINISM

What this category rejects — the historically limited archetype of womanhood — is necessarily more clear than what it is. Included amongst queer feminist representations are works made by artists who self-identify as women, though may not be a sexed female, heterosexual, or whose performance of the female gender does not readily play into a hetero-normative model of beauty or desire.

Despite her turn away from subversive visuals to promote her album, Joanne, Lady Gaga's early music videos make her one of the most prominent mainstream artists in this category. Videos such as... *Beautiful and Dirty Rich* and *Just Dance*, both released in 2008, present her as a carefree leader whose outlandish image and catchy choruses laid the foundation for the identity she continued to visually develop. Between 2009 and 2012, Lady Gaga released eleven music videos dominated by extravagant, defiant representations of gender and sexuality. In an interview in 2013, she reiterated statements made earlier in her career identifying her queer sexuality saying, "I like girls. I've said that. I know people think I just say things to be shocking, but I actually do like pussy."[6] Perhaps most indicative of a queer feminist approach to gender representation are her roles ranging from a lesbian prisoner making out with a fellow inmate in the 2010 video *Telephone*, to an androgynous, celibate, bionic widow turned nun in *Alejandro*, also released in 2010 [Figure 7], and a drag king, as her male persona, Joe Calderone in 2011's *Yoü and I* video [Figure 8].

Figure 7: Lady Gaga, *Alejandro*, 2010

Figure 8: Lady Gaga, *Yoü and I*, 2011

These works express the instability of binary gender categories (she plays not only man and woman but machine and mermaid in these videos), defy expectations of femininity and womanhood, and proliferate gender identities across the medium. These works also reinforce Butler's assertions that "the appearance of substance is simply a created identity."[7] Though Lady Gaga's core "substance" may be consistent across these identities, it is through performance that she defies the myth that gender identity is produced from that substance.

Vital to the production of these identities is the Artaudian strategy discussed earlier as one of the elements that unifies the work explored in this book. Artaud's brand of "extreme action pushed beyond limits,"[8] toward a severe production of thought "diligent and strict"[9] is dramatized by Lady Gaga in relation to the limits of gender norms. But, does Lady Gaga's own intellectual teleology mirror the perceived effects of her work? In considering Lady Gaga's own intentions, I would like to compare her performances of these characters with how she outlines the motivations behind her songwriting. She has said of writing the track "Born This Way" that she wanted to write her, "this-is-who-the-fuck-I-am anthem, an attack, an assault [...] Harkening back to the early '90s, when Madonna, En Vogue, Whitney Houston, and TLC were making very empowering music for women and the gay community and all kind of disenfranchised communities."[10] Her desire to make an "attack" reflects the severe theatrical approach of Artaud. Furthermore, what she strives for with this attack — a sense of empowerment for women, the gay community, and other disenfranchised communities — she also seeks to achieve in the subversive representations of gender and sexuality in the above examples of her videos. Lady Gaga's images and her expression of intentions to produce progressive social affect employ an Artaudian strategy crucial to actualizing Butler's theories.

The popular frenzy that Lady Gaga has incited over representational extremity, however, has produced new queer feminist scholarship as well. I see this as further evidence of Artaud's requirement of performance to produce thought. In *Gaga Feminism*, Jack Halberstam drafts a new credo of feminism inspired by Lady Gaga. They also assert that the landscape of popular culture is an historic and important battleground for queer activism — something understood by groups like the Mattachine Society and Daughters of Bilitis, and seized on by the gay liberation movement of the 1970s.[11] This thinking of the popular as politically potent reinforces popular music performance (and its modes of documentation, such as music video) as a crucial site for activating cultural change. Halberstam calls a feminism synthesized with pop culture in a post-Gaga society "a scavenger feminism" — "a politics that brings together meditations on fame and visibility with a lashing critique of the fixity of roles for males and females."[12] They see Lady Gaga as a symbol of the deterioration of classical sex systems and our collective inclination toward "preposterous" and "hallucinatory" alternative futures. [13]

This is, in fact, a feminism that readily chimes with my own creative objectives, as well as the music videos that I find most powerful. Regardless of the term's footing within universal discourse, this book is, to a significant degree, a "Gaga Feminist" project. Halberstam also locates the power to manipulate various facets of our identities culturally accepted as "givens," through performance. They explain by saying, "Lady Gaga [becomes] the vehicle for performing the very particular arrangement of bodies, genders, desires, communication, race, affect, and flow."[14] Halberstam deals with Gaga as the imitable representative that both announces the desire to undo cultural norms and sanctifies subversive performances in everyday life. This relates to the idea of the Carnivalesque. Halberstam deals with Gaga as a sort of beacon of radicality through which people might find their escape from normality. In a way, this reflects the idea of the Carnivalesque as being a momentary relief, which is enjoyed and resets our abilities to carry on the patterns of our responsibilities and roles. I want to be clear that I see subversive representations of gender within the popular cultural landscape as having contextual effects depending on the audience. What is subversive to a small town in Iowa may not seem subversive at all to a queer audience of drag queens in New York City. Despite discrepant effects, I have made my selection of examples not based on any impossible universal reception of some audience, but on the intentions of the performer — where they clearly deviate from norms, and, in the cases of most of the performers I observe, continue to exist, dress, perform, and think in ways that refuse those images and lifestyles from which the Carnivalesque offers only temporary respite.

Ultimately, *Gaga Feminism* is about the overlap between queer and popular culture, and how these issues get distilled down to a domestic and relatable cultural level. It uses Lady Gaga as a direct conduit to feminist theory, establishing her as an icon of sexual agency, confrontation, and progress, whose effects can be felt at common levels.

Gaga experiments with various incarnations of the

self, ultimately showing just how mutable and arbitrary a singular, definable "self" is, whether, male, female, or even human. While establishing the unfixed nature of gender and sexuality is paramount to Gaga's mission and performance, we might compare this to how other artists assert that it is their queer identity which must be considered fixed.

Peaches and the Gossip rose to prominence around the same time as Lady Gaga in 2008, but may be considered as having developed through earlier queer musical movements such as Riot Grrrl and Queer/Homocore. After building careers on independent labels such as Kill Rock Stars, K Records, and Mr. Lady — labels which have a history of supporting queer artists — several musicians and groups who are gay or have gay members were signed to major labels in the early 2000s. These artists included Peaches, the Gossip, Le Tigre, Tegan and Sara, and the Scissor Sisters. Peaches' *Talk to Me* video shows the singer in a leotard desperately begging and shouting at the camera, as she moves through an empty, dark, and eerie house, uncovering women in underwear wearing massive tangled wigs.

Piles of hair slowly take over whole sections of the house before Peaches is joined by all of her discovered women, sexually entangling herself in their bodies and hair. Feminist author Germaine Greer says that "[i]n the popular imagination, hairiness is like furriness, an index of bestiality, and as such an indication of aggressive sexuality."[15] She says that whereas men are encouraged to cultivate this, women are taught to shave, to suppress their bestiality, as they are their vigor and libido.[16] In Greer's context, Peaches can be seen as asserting her lesbian sexuality, vigor, and libido through the wild and abundant hair imagery.

The Gossip's video for *Move in the Right Direction* shows lesbian drummer Hannah Blilie enter the frame in a leather jacket, jeans, boots, and a buzz cut hairstyle, before taking her place at the drums to begin the song. I would like to explore Blilie's identity in dialogue with another of Halberstam's texts, *Female Masculinity*, which further contextualizes the fluid nature of masculinity and femininity between genders. Halberstam begins with a discussion of the formation of female identity. She explores how being a "tomboy" is accepted to a point, and then as soon as puberty begins, the full force of gender conformity descends on the girl — onto all girls, not just tomboys.[17] Halberstam frames the pressure of being boxed in in a way that foreshadows acts of extremity in representation — as if literally exploding out of these historical confines. Halberstam claims that, rather than an impersonation of maleness, female masculinity exposes yet another "performance" of gender. They question, however, why it is not accepted in the same way as it is when performed by men, despite women having made convincing "assaults on the coherence of male masculinity for over one hundred years."[18] Why do we continue to attribute masculinity to maleness?

Blilie's butch appearance can be counted as one of the assaults referenced by Halberstam — as a subversion of both the male and female gender — exposing masculinity as a performance, equally as adaptable by and applicable to the female sex. Despite referencing a history of masculine women, Halberstam explains that, "female masculinities are framed as the rejected scraps of dominant masculinity in order that male masculinity may appear to be the real thing."[19] To be a "real thing" would mean stemming from the male gender, whose performance of masculinity has been falsely naturalized.

In contrast to Blilie's female masculinity, lead singer Beth Ditto, a femme lesbian, is shown in heavy makeup and feminine dress. The collision of identities here is notable for its discrepant display of both masculinity and femininity by two women of the same sexuality. The video's entourage of male dancers further destabilizes the connection of masculinity to maleness. The dancers perform effeminate choreography and are dressed in futuristic, spandex with leather epaulettes and are dressed in futuristic, spandex body suits with leather epaulettes. These characters represent the lack of causality between maleness and masculinity.

Another destabilization of the sex/gender tie is seen through the work of Jeffree Star. Star was also signed to a major label after gaining popularity on the internet platform Myspace. Star is a gay male who dresses exclusively in ultra-feminine drag. Of drag performance, Butler has said, "drag fully subverts the distinction between inner and outer psychic space and effectively mocks both the expressive model of gender and the notion of a true gender identity."[20] Star's videos *Beauty Killer* and *Prom Night* are dominated by a pink palette of clothes, hair, and makeup, and showcase Star's myriad performances of femininity which reflect the subversive elements noted by Butler.

Unlike the artists above, cis-female performers such as Grimes and Paramore opt for a less glamorous and less sexualized aesthetic. In her video *Oblivion*, Grimes attacks hetero-male norms by both refusing standards of sexualized femininity and inserting herself in stereotypically hetero-male environments whose constructed performance is effectively highlighted by the already established performance context of the video. In the video, Grimes wears casual, punky clothes and her hair is dyed multiple colors. She is filmed singing the track in stadiums during an American football match and a motor-cross racing event. The shots cut-away to over-zealous fans watching the violent sports show; Grimes is a minority in the hyper-masculine environment to which she appears utterly indifferent. Perhaps the most interesting critique in the video comes through scenes of the men's locker room, where shirtless men covered only by white towels are shown lifting weights and examining themselves in slow motion. Several mirrors are included in the shot, and flashes of light go off as if referencing a camera's flash and the body cultivated to pose for it. Grimes exposes the privatization of male vanity — a trait more closely aligned with femininity and women. At the end of the video, Grimes is shown in a living room where shirtless men slam dance to her track. She adopts a stylized, though still unsexualized, feminine appearance. She wears a high-collared dress, which covers her arms, and is cut just above her knees. Her hair has been groomed out of its earlier-depicted frizzy and moppish state and she wears noticeable, if not heavy, makeup. Her presence is yet another subversion of the female role. She defies the limits associated with the feminine dress she adopts by positioning herself in the aggressive masculine environment.

Pop-punk band Paramore are another female-fronted act who generally eschew overt representations of sexuality. Paramore's videos often focus on live performance such as

Careful or *Ignorance*, showing lead singer Hayley Williams' energetic and highly physical delivery. She is portrayed not as masculine, but as boyish or a "tomboy." Williams has adopted a progressively more feminine appearance since the band's debut in 2007, though her performances and costuming in video have continued to avoid expressing sexual agency or desire.

The comparison of videos by the highly sexualized and feminine Lady Gaga and Peaches with those of Grimes and Paramore brings up issues about how the visibility and sexualization of bodies can be read as either objectification or sexual agency. Radical feminist Andrea Dworkin says that, "Objectification occurs when a human being, through social means, is made less than human, turned into a thing or commodity, bought and sold."[21] This in turn compromises their individuality and integrity. A generalized second-wave feminist reading of videos such as those by Gaga or Peaches would likely build off of Dworkin's definition to posit them as playing into patriarchal desire and commodifying sex in the same fell swoop as negating their interior value. While these artists have essentially made objects and, for that matter, brands of themselves ("Peaches" and "Gaga" being a bit more marketable sounding names perhaps, than Merrill Beth Nisker and Stefani Germanotta respectively), they have not made themselves "less human" as Dworkin suggests, but SuperHuman. When they yell into the camera and flaunt their bodies and sexuality, they do so with a conviction that renders them invincible. While Marsha Meskimmon acknowledges that, "[r]endering female sexual agency visible treads a dangerous path between an empowering investigation of desiring subjectivity and the objectification of 'woman' as no more than a sexual body,"[22] these images support her distinction that "representations of desire beyond the socially imposed limits of banal housewifery and sanitized prostitution can act against these restraints."[23]

Lady Gaga and Peaches are anything but representative of the banal housewife or any such antiquated female archetype. I am inclined to dismiss charges of objectification in videos such as these where the subversion of normative roles is pronounced alongside sexual agency. Sex is powerful, and both sexual agency and sexuality have been so grossly, historically policed that any provocative reiteration of a sexual self-possession is not only positive but symbolically necessary to a Western culture which is still flawed and dominated by hetero-sexist representations and norms. Grimes highlights the fact that sexual agency is not the only means at an artist's disposal for addressing issues of sexism, but perhaps the additional interplay of sexuality and sexual agency makes Lady Gaga's, and Peaches' work more complex and socially combative for operating on these additional, and more historically contentious, levels.

X. HOMO FEMININITY

This section observes works by feminine queer artists who also privilege their identity as gay cis-men. Mike Hadreas performs under the name Perfume Genius. The subversive elements in Hadreas' videos hit hard, carrying a sense of tragedy and frailty. *Hood* features gay pornstar Arpad Miklos, who fit Hadreas' desired casting description of someone "big, masculine, and tender."[24] Miklos is in fact burly, with a hairy chest, shaved head, and rippling muscles. Hadreas begins the song singing from Miklos' arms, in which he is cradled like an infant in a homoerotic Pietà. Miklos stares dotingly at Hadreas, who wears diamond cross-shaped earrings and a white mesh tank top, seemingly coupling gayness and purity. Miklos proceeds to slowly comb Hadreas' hair and apply makeup to his face. His hyper-masculine appearance and the hyper-sexual career for which he is known are subverted through incredibly tender and intimate acts of care. The couple then assumes various costumed poses while they stand for portraits indicated by the light from a camera's flash [Figure 9]. Hadreas elaborated on the video by saying,

[It's] about how if someone knew you 100%, they would go away [...] So, in the video, I didn't acknowledge him until I was fully done-up in all my gear and my wig. That's how I feel in general. That freaky shit underneath — that's kind of who I am, really.[25]

The struggle with identity that Hadreas expresses is not one of not knowing who he is, but of knowing and fearing that he will not be accepted by a partner for it — for, effectively, being too subversive. He represents this in an inverse way in the video by making his costumed, odd-looking self the one that he wishes to be seen.

Figure 9: Perfume Genius, *Hood*, 2012

Another of Hadreas' videos, *Take Me Home*, incorporates the same half-hearted, budget drag seen in *Hood*, though its darkness is enhanced by the isolation of Hadreas' character. The video opens with Hadreas lying in the street. He stands when a car rolls up to him, with its lights shining on his body. When he rises, we see Hadreas in hot pink high heels, stockings, a sports jersey with a large number four inscribed with the word "Play" (abbreviating "foreplay") in smaller lettering worn like a dress on his petite frame, a high school letterman-style sports jacket, and gold rings. Hadreas is followed by the car, as we are given the driver's view of him strutting slowly down the road. He then strikes fashion poses against a wall, spliced with shots from the industrial part of his hometown of Seattle. One shot focuses on Hadreas' knuckles displayed to the camera as a symbol of grit and self-protection (still decorated with feminine jeweled rings and painted nails), followed by a close-up of his arms crossed over his chest as he sways in a contrasting moment of tender, feminine, self-care. We see Hadreas enter a convenience store and emerge eating a Twinkie, referencing his gay identity as a "twink." Hadreas said that,

> *Take Me Home* carries a very desperate feeling. I'm walking around in a very hooker-y way. Truckers were whistling at me, which was both awesome and nerve-racking. There's a part of me that didn't really care, and there's another part of me that desperately hoped I was pulling it off.[26]

In the video, part of the desperation, which Hadreas notes above, and what I identify as subversive to the policing of gendered norms, comes from the commitment to portray this highly feminized, gay boy despite the clear destitution of his situation. This is compounded by Hadreas' quote, as he reveals his desire to satisfy the presumably hetero-male gaze of the truckers who witnessed his video shoot. Though the relationship between Hadreas' alignment of femininity, or perhaps more specifically homosexual femininity, with weakness and frailty is a tenuous one, the characters read more clearly as survivors rather than victims and present a more confessional sense of asserting one's gender and sexuality in a world dominated by hetero-sexist representation.

X. HOMO MASCULINITY

This section focuses on videos by gay cis-male artists who appropriate the hyper-masculine aesthetics historically aligned with heterosexual, often homophobic, cisgender male culture. These works subvert and contest the historical stereotype of gay men as effeminate and weak. However, in combatting this norm drawn from the alignment of homosexual men and heterosexual women for their shared desire of sexed-males, these images also contest the norm that heterosexual women should be feminine and are weak. In these works, stereotypical images of thugs, athletes, cowboys, and other masculine characters dominate, despite lyrical content or video narrative which pronounces the artists' homosexuality.

Until 2016, Frank Ocean was a notable exception in this category, as a cisgender, queer male artist who avoided queer imagery in his work. In a confessional narrative posted to social media site Tumblr in 2012, Ocean detailed his unrequited love and desire for a male friend. This preceded the release of his album, *Channel Orange*, where Ocean references his romantic interests with masculine pronouns. In "Thinkin Bout You," he croons, "My eyes don't shed tears, but boy they pour when I'm thinkin' 'bout you,"[27] and in the confessional, "Bad Religion," he laments, "This unrequited love, to me it's nothing but a one-man cult and cyanide in a Styrofoam cup, I could never make him love me."[28] Ocean revealed his sexuality only after signing with a major label and having an established fanbase with rap collective, Odd Future. This is to say: he was not an artist consciously signed and marketed with the interest of selling to an LGBTQ+ fanbase. Rather, his public outing subverted the image Odd Future had constructed of the boyish and vaguely violent,[29] if still artistic, indie skateboarding rap clan from Los Angeles. As the first, and one of the still very few mainstream rappers to be out as queer, Ocean's importance to defying the homophobic norms associated with rap culture cannot be overstated. I have specified that homophobia is widely associated with rap culture, rather than asserting that rap culture is homophobic, for as queer rapper Mykki Blanco has stated, "let's not be racist and target hip-hop! Why is the music business in general so homophobic?"[30] Blanco makes a strong point supported by the lack of queer artists in mainstream music. Though perhaps is it encouraging to note emerging rap artists such as Young Thug, who seem to be of a generation whose relationship to gender norms has shifted. Young Thug maintains a fluid gender style, sometimes wearing feminine clothes, such as the Alessandro Trincone couture dress worn on the cover of his album *Jeffery* [Figure 10]. Young Thug has also stated, "You could be a gangster with a dress or you could be a gangster with baggy pants. I feel like there's no such thing as gender."[31]

Figure 10: Young Thug, *Jeffery* Album Cover, 2016

He makes no clarification if someone might uphold the status of "gangster" regardless of sexuality rather than dress, though if Young Thug believes that gender does not exist, then presumably sexuality stands to be unhinged from the gender norms which have historically policed it. Rap and hip-hop have also seen a plethora of emerging queer artists changing the scope of the genres: Zebra Katz, TheeSatisfaction, Big Freedia, Brooke Candy, Angel Haze, Psycho-Egyptian, Le1f, Cakes da Killa, and Mykki Blanco. However, as Carrie Battan points out, the support for these rappers may only be part of a specific enclave whose perspective may not be shared by mainstream audiences. Battan says that, "acceptance for queer figures in rap outside of a New York underground bubble are still flimsy at best."[32] She also says that superficial references to gay acceptance must be reinforced with tangible actions at mainstream levels through live bills shared between gay and straight rappers, radio play, or label deals.[33]

Battan makes the point that mainstream rap has yet to put its supposed acceptance into more visual practice and to incorporate queer acts more significantly into its economy. She also notes the persistence of a homophobic mentality among top rap acts, such as A$AP Rocky, who, despite claiming acceptance, structures it around precariously worded caveats: "Man, if you're gay we can be friends [...] As long as you're a great person and, y'know, you don't bother me and make me uncomfortable, then let's be friends, dude."[34] In light of such quotes, Battan concludes that heterosexual rappers

> Cherry-pick gay culture for things [they] can use to enhance [their] own brand, fly [their] fashionable freak flag high, grandstand [their] anti-homophobic statements [...] and wait for the applause (it will come). But make sure to keep the gay men at a fearful arm's length at all times.[35]

Battan's suggestion that rappers flirt with queerness to the edge of its marketing potential and reserve collaboration and business for their "safe" hetero counterparts is what makes Frank Ocean's latest video work a significant step toward queering mainstream rap. Though gender subversion was not thematically prevalent in the images of Ocean's videos for songs from *Channel Orange*, the *Nikes* video — the first released in promotion of his next album, *Blond* — experiments with the queer representation of subjects in the video and Ocean's own queer identity.

The video opens with a shot of Ocean alone on stage. Lit by bright white lights from several angles, this first image of Ocean presents him as both ethereal and exposed. His face is covered in glitter and his white ensemble is feminized with heavy pearl embellishments [Figure 11]. Ocean's angelic appearance is both highlighted and juxtaposed by a devil character that appears later in the video, dancing in the upper balcony of the theater. The pairing reflects much of the video's concern with dueling sides or versions of the self.

Figure 11: Frank Ocean, *Nikes*, 2016

What follows is a series of low quality screen tests that show alternative-looking young people, perhaps auditioning for the video as later scenes suggest. The images' underproduced, unpretentious quality allows tattooed and pierced bodies to appear effortlessly natural. Their subtle queerness is expressed by a gentle refusal to produce gendered aesthetics and presumably their behavioral norms, or to exert similar energies on the cultivation of an appearance which directly contests them. These figures appear later at a party, which is revealed to be staged. At various points in the video, elements of the production itself — cameras, lighting rigs, clapperboards, footage from dress rehearsal — are exposed, maintaining an awareness of Ocean's lack of boundaries between personal and performative space, as well as the construction of performance and identity in both realms.

Following footage of the screen tests, Ocean is shown sitting outside in the dirt, leaning against the back of a numbered and branded race car. His casual, masculine dress of jeans, Nike trainers, and a heavy, army green coat, and the rugged environment around him contrasts the softer image of Ocean previously shown in established artistic space. However, the masculinity of the image is also subverted by his dramatic eye makeup, which suggests he is of the same alternative enclave as the group pictured in the screen tests. He drinks from a disposable cup, then stumbles, presumably from inebriation. As if an effect of the alcohol, the song's vocal is slowed to the point of distortion. He repeats, "I've got two versions," again reinforcing the sense of a split self he has introduced by pairing angelic and satanic images and exploring a sense of his on- and off-stage self. Two statues of the Virgin Mary are shown in the back seat of a moving car, suggesting we are meant to hear, "I've got two virgins," in Ocean's looped, effected vocal. Two young, Asian women, wearing stereotypically fetishized school uniforms displace the statutes. Are these the virgins he references? The continual reference to "two versions" proposes a dichotomy between Ocean's personas, which is further highlighted by the interplay of images such as these "two versions" of virgins. On stage, he appears glowing, safe and calm under theater lights. Off stage we see him stumbling, drunk, somewhat desperate, perhaps seeking to reconcile his queerness with a masculinity historically aligned with male heterosexuality.

In the subsequent shots, Ocean's reality becomes distorted and pieced together as if recalling a dream, or perhaps constructing a queer fantasy. Perhaps these are the images Ocean sees when he closes his eyes on stage, while putting forth the persona of the seraphic star. The camera moves up the legs of a black body laid on a floor of dollar bills. The shot moves overhead at such a distance that the gender of the figure remains obscured. With this shot, Ocean plays with our established notions of desire. Is attraction to this svelte, oiled, erotic figure to be withheld until their gender is confirmed? The scene shifts with the addition of a second body. A black man's manicured red nails are shown caressing his chest, subverting masculine norms. His head rests on the belly of his female doppelganger. We are again presented with the concept of "two versions" — one male, one female, with similar, and equally eroticized bodies. It remains unclear which figure we were first introduced to, but the image suggests gender as an irrelevant factor in producing desire.

Later scenes continue to conflate satanic and angelic imagery with sexuality and gender roles, consistently abiding by the video's sense of duality. A black male stripper is shown holding onto a pole in black angel wings. The figure may actually be Ocean. He wears the same heavy black eye makeup shown in the earlier outdoor scene. Perhaps this is his second, sexual, queer version of himself: a darker foil to the angelic version of Ocean first presented. The video concludes with Ocean setting himself on fire, as if suggesting he is in hell. The moral entanglements of gender and sexuality are further evoked when Ocean appears in a rare shirt designed by artist Jenny Holzer for her Truisms series in 1987 [Figure 12]. Among the phrases printed on shirt are, "raise boys and girls the same way," "salvation can't be bought and sold," "nothing upsets the balance of good and evil," and "random mating is good for debunking sex myths."

These images do not clarify the specific queerness of Ocean's sexuality. Rather, the video hints at his struggle to navigate the moral perceptions of sexuality between public and private life, or the absence of such boundaries at his level of visibility. Ocean has remained fairly ambiguous about his sexuality since his Tumblr post, despite drawing consistent media attention. *Nikes* seems to address a period of inner turmoil — a somewhat expected, or unsurprising subtext given Ocean's public scrutiny.

Figure 12: Frank Ocean, *Nikes*, 2016

In the less commercial rap world is Lelf, an artist formerly signed to a subsidiary label of the independent XL Recordings. Homosexuality and a masculine expression of homoerotic desire is Lelf's focus in much of his work, including in the video *Soda*. In the video, two men confront each other in a stare-down wearing casual black outfits. One man's shirt is open, and the other's is made of diaphanous mesh, suggesting the sexual nature of their encounter. Two fake products — a large bottle of soda and a tube of candy — are respectively marked "Lelf" and "Boody" (the name of the track's co-producer). The two men combine the soda and candy, causing the soda to fizz. The effect is exaggerated in the video, as soda spouts and flows in slow motion over the two men's faces, who relish in the moment, alluding to ejaculation with closed eyes and open mouths. The assertion here is that, when combined, Lelf and Boody will make you cum. Before proceeding, I will note that my reading of this work differs slightly from that of Stan Hawkins, author of *Queerness in Pop Music*. In his book,

Hawkins claims that Le1f "denigrates the character and iconography of the tough, worked-out masculine rapper,"[36] and that this both "contests the homophobic tendencies in hip hop"[37] and "strips down the rigid structures of masculinity with the aid of exclusive haute couture."[38]

I agree with Hawkins that Le1f differs in appearance from certain stereotypes of "straight, macho, worked-out" rappers, perhaps alluding to artists such as Jay-Z, Lil Wayne, or Eminem. However, I do not agree that Le1f's clothes obscure or dismantle his masculinity. This simple difference in our observation of gendered aesthetics bares significant implications for the argument of this section. I view Le1f's use of masculine aesthetics in this work as an intentional play to unhinge masculinity from the heterosexual male figure to which it has historically been anchored, and from which it has been falsely thought to have been produced. It is precisely the unfixed nature of masculinity that I seek to establish in this reading of *Soda*. Le1f's high fashion costumes seem to draw inspiration from Andre 3000 (of rap duo Outkast), share a sartorial attention to some of Kanye West's more elaborate tour ensembles designed by Maison Martin Margiela, and are considerably less flamboyant than the costumes of performers such as Gnarls Barkley singer Ceelo Green [Figure 13, 14, 15, 16].[39] Though Hawkins might also interpret these artists' appearances as unmasculine, or threatening to masculinity, his failure to contextualize Le1f among these or similar artists implies that Le1f's unmasculine appearance derives from his queer identity.

Figure 13: Andre 3000 of Outkast on *The Tonight Show*, 2002

Figure 14: Le1f, *Soda*, 2012

Figure 15: Kanye West, Multiple costumes featured
throughout the *Yeezus* tour, (2013–14)

Figure 16: Ceelo Green, Performance ensembles
featured on *The Voice* (2011–13)

My assertion that Lelf's masculine appearance expresses the unfixed nature of masculinity might be further supported by an observation Hawkins fails to make. One of the dancers with whom Lelf is shown throughout the video is Juliana Huxtable, a transgender artist, author, and member of New York arts collective House of Ladosha. Huxtable Vogues in a high-fashion, structural ensemble of iridescent bustier and skirt. Her placement highlights Lelf's comparable masculinity [Figure 17], despite the fact that Huxtable's trans identity and representation also further serves the overriding thesis that gender is neither fixed nor inherently tied to a masculine or feminine aesthetic. I also agree with Hawkins that Lelf destabilizes norms and contests homophobia, though I see the homoerotic scenes of the video that follow as better examples to support such claims.

Figure 17: Lelf, *Soda*, 2012

Lelf re-visits the soda imagery in another shot where three figures stand over a feminine, bearded man with long hair, pouring soda on him. As with the video's opening encounter between two men, this shot is again in slow motion, adding drama to the ritualistic scene. The shot references a golden shower. With the exception of Huxtable, whose dress is readably "femme," Lelf and the other characters are styled in avant-garde fashions that appropriate masculine garments. Lelf wears two pieces of an American football uniform — spandex pants padded at the knees and thighs and a cropped sports shirt, which has been made of denim. Sex is the subtext of *Soda*, specifically gay sex and deviant sex acts, which Lelf manages to align with masculinity through costuming and a juxtaposition with feminized queer counterparts.

Lelf uses the same tactic in the video *Hush Bb*. In this work, he shares a moody and romantic room filled with candles, a vanity, blue roses, and a bed covered in dark satin sheets with a young woman with long blonde hair, wearing a leotard. The camera subtly displaces the characters into the other's position throughout the video, highlighting a masculine/feminine exchange. They prepare themselves while seated in front of the vanity or grind and gyrate slowly over the satin sheets in the background. The sexualized actions are leveled as neither specifically male or female, despite the clearly defined masculine and feminine aesthetics of Lelf and his female counterpart respectively. As in *Soda*, Lelf makes further reference to ejaculation and insemination. He pours honey into a cup, holding one receptacle high above the other to exaggerate the act. The woman repeats the motion when she is placed in Lelf's position at the vanity, again marking sexual desire as independent of gender. Lelf reinforces his gay identity through his indifference to the girl's sexual, bodily display, yet his masculinity is highlighted in juxtaposition with her femininity.

Mykki Blanco is another gay, sexed-male rapper whose inclusion in this category is somewhat tenuous for their historically fluid gender identity. But before exploring Blanco's work, I must refute another alignment drawn by Hawkins, who claims that some of the direct influences on Blanco and other of their contemporaries, such as queer black rapper Zebra Katz, include the coming out of mainstream artists such as Frank Ocean and Azealia Banks, and ball culture.[40]

I see little correlation amongst the artists Hawkins draws together. Hawkins views Blanco's open expressions of queerness as inspired by the more mainstream figure of Frank Ocean. This is a marginalization of Blanco on several fronts. By the time Ocean released the letter online which delicately, if not ambiguously, addressed his sexuality in 2012, Blanco was living as a transgender woman, was a published author, and emerging as a buzzworthy artist, touring with established rap/noise act Death Grips. Hawkins also maintains that Blanco's identity stems from ball culture, which Blanco directly refutes:

> I did not start in the drag community. Mykki Blanco began because I was actually, for the first time, having a bit of my own sexual revolution — I started cross-dressing and living a transgender lifestyle. Mykki Blanco came out of that, but it wasn't a lineage of drag performance.[41]

In addition to the above assertion that Blanco does not identify with the drag community, Blanco further distances themselves from ball culture, and identifies the cultural movements with which they do identify by saying, "You can't tag me as the rapping transvestite. I never Vogued in my life. I'm from a punk and Riot Grrrl background."[42] Hawkins aligns Blanco's success with Ocean's despite their highly discrepant musical styles, and the fact that Blanco was gaining notoriety even before Ocean publicly addressed his sexuality. Hawkins also wrongly asserts that Blanco was inspired by ball culture, whose foundations of drag and glamor starkly contrast the subcultural dogma of punk and Riot Grrrl, whose tenets are rooted in DIY politics and non-conformity. Hawkins does later mention Blanco's ties to punk movements, but in the same passage again asserts that Blanco is inspired by mainstream artists:

> Blanco's identity is inspired by mainstream artists such as Rihanna, Lauryn Hill, and Lil' Kim, as well as the entire Queercore and Riot Grrrl movement. There are also overt references to the drag queen, Vaginal Davis, and the controversial Canadian director and writer, Bruce LaBruce.[43]

In the above section, Hawkins has conflated several artists and subcultures, only categorically unified as queer, black, and performative. Though this passage notes Blanco's interest in Riot Grrrl, which Blanco has directly affirmed, attributing influence to pop stars such as Rihanna contradicts Blanco's punk ethos. In several other interviews, Blanco has also said that they wanted to be "the next Yoko Ono,"[44] reinforcing their desired identity to be a performance artist, rather than one of the more commercial and glamorous figures which ball culture emulates, and that Rihanna simply *is*. And, while

Blanco does share an aesthetic with Davis, Hawkins calls Davis a "drag queen" without elaborating on the fact that Davis, like Blanco, critiques drag culture (and the culture it imitates) rather than participating in its conventional lineage. Reinforcing this interpretation of Davis' work, José Muñoz has called Davis' performances "terrorist drag," "insofar as she is performing [America]'s internal terrors around race, gender, and sexuality."[45] Because drag performance typically imitates established standards of beauty and femininity, Muñoz's quote suggests the fear of those standards being appropriated and corrupted by a figure whose doubly marginalized status as black and queer confronts the racist, hetero-sexist infrastructure of those standards. Hawkins also draws no specific examples from LaBruce's oeuvre in order to affirm his connection to Blanco. In clarifying the subcultures and artists with whom Blanco most closely identifies, it is my intention to read accurate motives within the work.

In the video *Wavvy* Blanco meets a drug dealer in downtown New York wearing a backwards baseball cap, no shirt, and slim cut jeans. The jeans are a feminine pastel pink, but are filthy and ripped at the knee, signifying a masculine grit (again, and as ever, not a *male* grit. Masculinity and femininity remain unhinged from sex). Blanco's nails are painted, but chipped. They rap half the song in masculine street attire before switching to a posh club scene, wearing a wig, bikini-style underwear, layered rhinestone belts, and heels.

Blanco leaves their chest bare, not attempting to hide their male physique. The party is filled with other guests in formal attire and men in full drag and makeup. The cut-away shots of Blanco in masculine dress, rapping in the back of a large truck, highlight issues of class — that it is essentially safe to cross-dress amongst an upper-class, art party crowd, and not acceptable within lower-class street culture. This is supported by Railton and Watson, who point out the commonly-argued idea that "it is precisely the commodification of feminism [...] that recasts the image of the modern feminist from a political identity into a consumer choice [...] postfeminism becomes [...] reduced to images of successful women."[46] Railton and Watson critique an image of a postfeminist world where designer clothes or other expensive goods express power and position, and are indicative of a feminist approach, or that feminism has succeeded in opening male-dominated industries, where women might now compete. Railton and Watson suggest that feminism is essentially for sale: transformed from a belief and practice that combats exclusionary politics based on gender into its own exclusionary politics based on class. Blanco's relegation of their feminist persona to the upper-class milieu reinforces this. This is further echoed by Blanco's inclusion of an obese woman in her underwear at the party, who, like Blanco, does not meet conventional standards of feminine beauty, but who can express freedom of sex and sexuality in a world of pre-existing privilege.

In the video *The Initiation,* Blanco abandons feminine aesthetics entirely, with the exception of a shot of their painted nails in the opening. The video is intensely violent, with a dark, masculine aesthetic. Blanco wears black jeans and a ripped black t-shirt; and crawls toward the camera. Video of Blanco's face has been superimposed onto their forehead, so that they retain eye contact with the camera while their actual, non-digitized face is lowered to the ground [Figure 18].

Figure 18: Mykki Blanco, *The Initiation*, 2013

Blanco arrives at a bunker after passing through an industrial landscape. After entering a room sectioned off with cage wire, they remove their shirt and re-assume their crawling position. Blanco is matched with a shirtless black, cisgender male, who has the same facial animation on his head. The two brawl, and Blanco is shown bludgeoning the man while blood spouts towards the camera. Blanco is paid for the victory, and throws cash upon the victim in an act of disrespect.

Coming from an artist so aware of their gay/trans persona, the masculine violence — similar to what we observed earlier through Le1f's masculine aesthetics — subverts the perception of gay men as effeminate and "less than," while also tapping into the homoeroticism of sweating, aggressive, wrestling bodies; further suggesting the broader homo-eroticism of organized male sport. For those already familiar with Blanco's oeuvre, or those who pick up on the artist's painted nails as an establishment of their queer identity, the video's violence subverts the idea of gay men as weak. The video otherwise mocks the audience who misses these elements — a veritable parody of how violence has been thought to authenticate heterosexual manhood.

While Le1f and Blanco seem to draw on stereotypical masculine images of "jocks" and "thugs" respectively, gay, male, solo electronic and pop artist SSION appropriates the masculine figure of a cowboy in his video *Earthquake*. In this work, SSION exaggerates and glorifies his specifically gay masculinity, while directly attacking hetero-conventions, aesthetics, and roles as limited and boring. The video begins with a long shot of a house on an open plot of green land. Its classic suburban appearance is symbolic of both the typical American model of family and security, as well as the mass-produced uniformity of that model. A red pickup truck circles the house and is shown driving directly over a rose bush. The camera pans up to show SSION singing into a red landline receiver from the truck, while directly addressing the camera. The pickup truck acts as a symbol of his masculinity, compounded by its crushing of another symbol of femininity and love. SSION also wears a masculine cowboy ensemble, subverted by his made-up face with lipstick and eyeshadow, painted nails, and rhinestone jewelry [Figure 19]. The image of him talking on the phone is shown streaming into the bedroom of a character who we presume is speaking to SSION, as he is also shown holding a landline receiver in bed. The boy wears an outlandish outfit of a slightly acid house aesthetic, with checkered pants and a black-and-white tube top over a long-sleeved yellow shirt. He is bald with a thin mustache that draws comparison to iconic gay filmmaker John Waters [Figure 20].

Figure 19: SSION, *Earthquake*, 2012

Figure 20: SSION, *Earthquake*, 2012

This character plays the homoerotic object of SSION's desire throughout the video. His maudlin demeanor symbolizes the difficult navigation of boundaries imposed by conventional binaries and social structures as he tries to unite with SSION. After his father is shown nodding off while watching television, the boy is driven by his mother and her friend, who exemplify stereotypes of frumpy house-wives, through a nondescript suburban neighborhood. He is dropped off at a school where mythical characters such as Cupid, Santa Claus, The Wicked Witch of the West, and the Easter Bunny are shown watching SSION videos, shaving in the bathroom, or mopping the floor, as if to assert that high schools, America, and the suburban ideological landscape at large are where social myths and stereotypes are housed and likely created. The exaggeration of gender stereotypes in the video suggests that such myth-making might extend to gender and sexuality as well. The boy enters two double doors with the word "Come" on the outside, subversively referencing ejaculation. He enters to find SSION performing in front of large letters that spell out "H-O-M-E." This moment has a three-fold effect of pairing with the sign on the door to say "come home," implying safety, and SSION's invitation to the boy, and also referencing the words "Homme" — "man" in French — and "Homo" — a reiteration of their sexuality. This video, like those above, makes violent attacks on hetero-masculinity, revealing how easily it is performed regardless of sexuality, and that it is in fact a crucial element of the identity of the above-mentioned artists' queer sexual allure.

X. CYBORG FEMINISM

This section explores videos whose post- and non-human aesthetics strategically subvert masculine and feminine appearances and roles through a broader subversion of the human form. Unlike androgynous representations, which typically combine masculine and feminine traits, the figures in these works eschew the very human characteristics from which these categories are derived. Instead, they often adopt the appearance of animals, machines, or both. Even in the instances we will explore where gender is determinable, the focus is often still placed on cultivating an identity independent of the framework of sex — such as that of the cyborg.

These images propose nuanced questions that differ in significant way from images that abide by human representation. Has contemporary technology served as a feminist tool? Are these posthuman representations a feminist subversion of gender categories, or does their abandonment of gendered aesthetics also sacrifice a position of commentary on gender? Do these elaborate representations expose masculinity and femininity as fabrications of comparable fantasy? We will also consider how a technological backlash may be responsible for the elaborate biomorphic representations of artists such as Björk. Let us begin by unpacking some of the posthuman discourse that helps frame the view of these works.

In Katherine Hayles' *How We Became Posthuman* she explains, "Although the 'posthuman' differs in its articulations, a common theme is the union of the human with the intelligent machine."[47] What may once have been a fantasy of science fiction is now close to reality. In our Western post-internet era we are often tethered, if not yet fully hardwired, to the clever mobile devices that relentlessly deliver us texts, emails, reminders, news, photos, songs, and a plethora of other media and information. As the internet and the technology required to access it have become fundamental to our contemporary mode of being, articulations of the cyborg have been explored to feminist effect in music video.

One of the ways in which this has been executed is through a glamorization of technology, where artists embellish themselves with machine-like accessories, reinforcing an image of modernity and intelligence. Brooke Candy clads herself in gold metallic armor akin to that of the *Star Wars* humanoid C-3PO in her video *Das Me*, and wears a silver version of the robotic suit when featuring as a character in Grimes' video *Genesis*. Similarly glamorized is Lady Gaga's complete cyborg becoming in her video for *Yoü and I*. The video opens with a long shot of Gaga walking down a paved road in an elaborate ensemble of all black with massive round, metallic, silver sunglasses, and a large, round hat with a black veil. Juxtaposed with the green fields flanking the pavement, Gaga is made to look intentionally alien — a fact later affirmed by the various incarnations of her character throughout the video, including mermaid and winged creature. The camera moves briefly to a shot of her feet, which are bloodied and covered in dirt. As the character removes some debris from its heels, the shot reveals a bionic limb. A montage ensues of her in various states of construction by a male counterpart, played by Gaga's former partner Taylor Kinney. The scene references Mary Shelley's *Frankenstein*, affirming that Gaga is a creation, rather than a natural being. A longer shot of the bionic Gaga reveals that the mechanism previously shown on her hand travels the full length of her arm and around her neck and ear [Figure 21]. Wiring protrudes from her shoulder, denying the totality of her human and thus female state. A metal plate also appears to have been drilled into Gaga's chin, indicated by drops of blood surrounding the area.

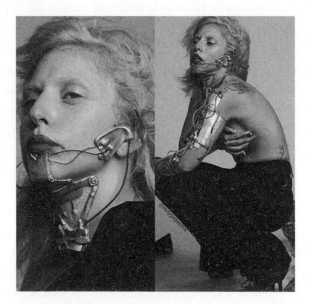

Figure 21: Detail of costume in Lady Gaga's
Yoü and I video, 2011

This suggestion of enduring the painful installation of these technological prostheses reinforces the idea of her desensitized cyborg self. Donna Haraway proposes the feminist value of cyborg representation by saying that it suggests a way out of the maze of dualisms in which we have explained our bodies.[48] Haraway reiterates a break with the duality of gender and a way to appropriate and re-inscribe the body through the cyborg, which Gaga exemplifies.

Though technology's connotations of intelligence, ingenuity, and modernity are aspects of what reinforces the above-mentioned artists' cyborg imagery as feminist, we might also consider how technology is being put in service of a contemporary glamor. The work of Carol Dyhouse offers a potential response via the historic idea of glamor, which she qualifies as powerfully transformative. Rather than a restrictive or prescriptive aesthetic, Dyhouse claims that a desire for glamor represents an audacious refusal to be imprisoned by norms of class and gender or by expectations of conventional femininity; it is defiance rather than compliance, a boldness which might be seen as unfeminine.[49]

The glamorous iterations of the feminist cyborg fully reinforce Dyhouse's characterization of glamor as a progressive vehicle. Artists such as Brooke Candy and Lady Gaga glamorize and mystify themselves through cyborg personas whose feminist impulse is tied to the intelligence and power deflected by their machine state.

However, these works also propose a question posed by Paula Rabinowitz: "In claiming space for the posthuman are we erasing yet again women's lives and stories?"[50]

Rabinowitz suggests that perhaps the female body requires greater political visibility before it is obscured by the posthuman. Rabinowitz's question can also be asked of queer representation or the representation of other marginalized groups. This, indeed, draws us into further concerns about what constitutes womanhood, feminism, queerness, or whether queerness always includes feminism, or vice versa. I would like to explore this in relation to London-based Venezuelan electronic artist Arca's most recent suite of videos as compared to their earlier video work.

Arca's videos have always been of interest to me, but typically lacked the kind of additional images or narrative that might complicate and contextualize relationships, environments, and identities. They often focused on a single image — either Arca's body, or a computer-animated figure of ambiguous gender — moving in vaguely sexual manner. In *Sad Bitch* we see a digital figure, naked, with an oleaginous, variegated green skin dancing slowly from behind. Small red bursts explode out of their back to the beat, then linger and float around their form. The figure's back appears polyped and grotesque as more starry red bursts accumulate in the frame. The figure in *Thievery* is similar; digital, naked, bald, and androgynous, with the same sickly skin color. We again see them from behind as they dance, but this figure shakes their ass, twerks, and squats to the floor with their knees spread and their hands above their head. This figure eventually faces the camera, revealing breasts, but amorphous genitalia, which defy our initial inclination to gender the figure female. Close stills of the forward-facing body reveal demonic, child-like faces, inset in the figure's hips. These are some of director Jesse

Kanda's signature characters. The video *Soichiro* marked
a turning point for the inclusion of Arca's body, but still
lacked broader context. Arca's recent works, however,
have included more homoerotic and feminine imagery and
costumes. These aesthetics have been compounded with
images of wounds, prosthetics, and fusions with machine,
suggesting an invincibility. This culminates in a posthuman
feminism, enacted on a body further signified as queer
through performances in the video which I will explain
below. This work seems to defy the erasure that Rabinowitz
identifies as a potential byproduct of the posthuman.

In *Reverie,* we first see Arca's hand protruding from a
heavy, white lace sleeve of a bullfighter's jacket. A small
bit of torn fabric hangs from the cuff, set against a hot pink
background. The delicate lace and saturated color read of
the classically feminine. The shot slowly moves up and
away from their body, revealing complicated leg prosthetics.
The attachments are made of leather and metal rods and
are modeled after a bull's leg shape. Arca's feet are held in a
stirrup of each attachment and they stand on metal hooves.
Around the knee, there is a white globular shape, the
texture of which is bumpy, covered in a lacey black fabric,
and vaguely reptilian. The construction of the attachment
gives the illusion that this is Arca's exposed skin. They wear
black thong underwear. As the shot pulls further back we
see that Arca is in an abstract space with neon red floors,
flanked by curving hot pink walls. A sudden close-up on
Arca's face shows them in unexpected anguish. They look
up with eyes wide and mouth drawn. The camera moves
to the level of their pelvis. Another close shot shows that
they have been penetrated from behind, straight through

their body by a bull's horn. As Arca grapples with the horn, however, the image looks simultaneously masturbatory. When the camera returns to their face, the suggestion of sexual pleasure gives a new reading to their expression. The image also readily suggests queer sexual penetration. Arca staggers away, grabbing their buttock, which is smeared with the blood from their wound. They collapse, and the light changes to dark blue. They begin to crawl, and flower petals descend upon them. Their backlit, slow-moving body now looks wiry and animal-like. The music surges again, and they stand in a kind of resurrection. The pink hues return to the light. They flail and reach their arm out while the shot staggers as if the Earth too is in a quivering state of trauma. They collapse for a final time against the bright pink stage, the song ends, and the shot cuts to black. Sexual pain and pleasure, masturbation, and queer sex are weighted with a valor imbued by their character as bullfighter. The elements' collision with, and subversion of the classically feminine aesthetics of pinks and lace affirm a queer feminist subtext. There is further gender dissonance proposed throughout, in the pairing of Arca's high, feminine, and operatic vocal with the more aggressive, industrial electronic sounds of the track. Arca has addressed this layered meaning, saying of the video that, "Bullfighting is a piercing metaphor: you are fighting a bull, and at the same [time] yourself. You are not the victim or the oppressor, you are both — Animality and bestiality are conflated. Evoking sex invokes our animality."[51]

In this work, they employ more direct human manipulation, still coded with a cyborg aesthetic. I propose that Arca's earlier work is less subversive, and ultimately less potent as queer and feminist work because it was symbolic of the posthuman, but ultimately always already non-human, un-human, digital. In a video such as *Reverie*, Arca displays the confusion and obliteration of the binary through the distinct production and performance of a live— aesthetically queer, feminist—posthuman other. For a scholar such as Robin Roberts, the body subsumed by technology in *Sad Bitch* (rather than embellished with glamorous, machine-like technology) would be seen as sufficiently subversive in its own right. In her book *Ladies First: Women in Music Video*, Roberts asks, "How can the deconstructive possibilities of the postmodern art form be harnessed for the subversive agenda of a feminism committed to questioning the traditional limits of femininity?"[52] In response, she explores the denaturalization of the cis-female body through montage, rapid sequencing, and fragmentation as combatting beauty and passivity as naturally feminine. She also sees this as working toward a confrontation with the commercial commodification of women's bodies in videos such as Pat Benatar's *Sex as a Weapon*, where Benatar performs against a satirical background of dozens of TV screens of leggy models.

Though this book is concerned with performance as the means of subverting traditional agendas, I agree with her focus on the form as its own source of discourse. This manipulation and mastery of the virtual anatomy also echoes a tenant of Hayles' definition of the posthuman. She calls the body "an original prosthesis we all learn to manipulate, so that extending or replacing the body with other prostheses becomes a continuation of a process that began before we were born."[53] I propose that our manipulation of, and reliance upon, technology has become, as Hayles suggests, a continuation of the prosthetic manipulation we first apply to our bodies. As Roberts' work shows, it can also be used to combat the limits of what those bodies signify.

The implications of such technological prosthesis are explored in Björk's video for *Pagan Poetry*. The video abstracts a sexual encounter; the intimate and kinetic are re-inscribed as mechanical and detached, though without compromise to aesthetic. The video proposes intimacy's invasion by, or perhaps assimilation with, technology. In the video a posthuman veil is applied to the graphic (human) sexual encounter between Björk and her then-partner, artist Matthew Barney. These scenes were filmed by Björk using a camera given to her by the video's director, Nick Knight. Our relationship to sexual norms is subverted through the intervention of technology. These scenes, which are abstracted through video effects that seem to solarize and map the skin in a network of thin lines, can still be deciphered as documenting various states of penetration and emission. And though we know from Knight's interview that it is a heterosexual encounter, it is leveled genderless through the technological abstraction.

In the video, Björk's body is sexually penetrated by her lover and later by herself in subversive acts of physical embellishment. She sews pearls onto her skin and receives multiple piercings in her back, from which even more strands of pearls are suspended in a lattice. Though the initial scenes of computerized pornography are the kind of posthuman provocations informing this text, I am interested in the latter image as it relates to Halberstam's definition of the posthuman as a "solidarity between disenchanted liberal subjects and those who were always-already disenchanted, those who seek to betray identities that legitimise or de-legitimise them at too high a cost."[54]

Halberstam suggests that one might *become* posthuman by betraying their legitimizing identities. As documented in the video, Björk makes this kind of posthuman transformation visible. She betrays or subverts classical expectations of femininity by fusing beauty with violence and pain. Further, it is revealed that these embellishments are part of a wedding costume. Björk's upper body is exposed, with a minimal scattering of the pearl embellishments. Below her exposed breasts is a more elaborate white garment designed by Alexander McQueen — a designer known for unconventional constructions that question standards of beauty. The latter half of the video shows only Björk giving a confrontational and emotive performance to the camera, where the vocals wail, then go a cappella, repeatedly declaring "I love him." Björk plays a sexual bride, subverting the most feminine of gender icons through scenes that border on the pornographic and masochistic. That border is constructed through the intervention of technology, changing our relationship to the intimate, erotic, and the painful

I would also like to consider how the non-human handling of gender may be a reaction to the posthuman inclination toward the technological. Björk's *Unravel* and *Oceania* are examples of the non-human that rely on fantasy, though are separate from futurity. They further echo Artaud's belief that, "from time to time cataclysms occur which compel us to return to nature i.e.: to rediscover life [...] animals, stones [...] costumes impregnated with bestial essences."[55] Artaud sees a return to nature as a return to life that Björk herself obscures through the digital landscape in *Pagan Poetry*. By comparison, *Unravel* and *Oceania* deal in aquatic, biomorphic aesthetics. In *Unravel*, tentacle-like, white strings appear wavering against an ambiguous black background. It is initially unclear whether they are in the depths of the sea or outer space. Fluttering electronic sounds and rich and resonant cello chords are layered before Björk's tender vocal enters, lending the space a sense of romance and security. The camera follows the strings back to their source: a round, black formation similar to a sea urchin, whose texture, however, is more like fur or hair. At its center are vaginal lips. The urchin is attached to Björk's body, who gently rocks with her legs tucked beneath her. She is costumed in a feminine, white, lace mini-dress, and directs the strings with her intricate hand gestures. It is difficult to say whether Björk, or her seemingly symbiotic attachment, is the source of these appendages, or if we might say that she has been penetrated by them. On the other end of the tentacles is a faceless, CGI sea creature resembling a jellyfish, squid, and cuttlefish. It dwarfs her form in size, and swirls in a black aquatic space. With these fantastical images, Björk exemplifies anther iteration of the posthuman that rejects the technological, while still inherently obscuring gender through an erasure of the human.

This is continued in *Oceania*, where Björk looks even more alien. Her face has been covered in glimmering gems. The bottom half of her body is either absent or obscured by her dark aquatic habitat. She emits jellyfish from her palms, which rise to a large network of orchid-like sea flowers.

In *Unravel* and *Oceania*, Björk is either augmented with symbiotic sea forms, or of a decidedly inhuman origin and habitat. A human inclination remains within these works, however; towards beauty and stylization.

I would like to conclude with a divergent view of the posthuman offered by Halbertam in their book *Posthuman Bodies*. They define the posthuman as accounting for the literal bodies that fall outside some socially determined mode of human fitness. They are failing, or they are changing (genders, for example), and they may not be accepted because of it. Further examples cited include

> queer, cyborg, metametazoan, hybrid, PWA; bodies-without-organs, bodies-in-process, virtual bodies: in unvisualizable amniotic indeterminacy, and unfazed by the hype of their always premature and redundant annunciation, who thrive in the mutual deformations of totem and taxonomy.[56]

I argue, however, that failure is precisely human: death, disease, vulnerability, as well as the host of emotions we feel through these experiences. Though the text draws potent insights into queer culture and queer bodies through the conduit of the posthuman topic, the relationship drawn from the posthuman term feels largely forced. *Posthuman Bodies* also remains generally less relevant to this book's focus on the elements of futurity and fantasy found mirrored more significantly in the work of Hayles and Haraway.

The value of fantasies such as the cyborg is echoed by Judith Butler in her essay, "The Force of Fantasy: Feminism, Mapplethorpe, and Discursive Excess." Butler explores fantasy as a means of achieving an unrealized futurity.

She says that "feminist theory relies on the capacity to postulate through fantasy a future that is [...] not equated with what is not real, but what is not yet real."[57]

Anchored to these fantastical representations, however, are the inescapable implications and questions of a posthuman existence. As Rabinowitz asks: "Do posthuman bodies *have* histories, genders, or sexualities?"[58] While the fantastic fictions created in music video find a way out of the restrictive confines of gender, the mythic taxonomy of cyborgs are all still ultimately human-made.

The works explored in this section, however, make posthuman discourse visible. Some of these works pull our relationship to technology into view, and others seem to reject that relationship through an exploration of more natural aesthetics. The fantastical performances and personae addressed above expose the illusion of our gendered aesthetics and inspire a means of their manipulation. Sexuality is necessarily a similar victim of this expository subversion. Biomorphic, cyborg, or other such post- and non-human representations level the gender system against a futurity where we are not fixed to our human identities.

X. THE SOFT BOYS

The work discussed thus far has shown that female and queer artists may subvert the expectations of gender and critique the gender binary by expressing gendered sexual empowerment, appropriating dress historically assigned to a specific gender, or by adopting biomorphic or bionic costume where gender is entirely obscured. There is an absence of this kind of subversion in videos by cisgender male artists who do not identify as queer. An exception to this is found in the video work of rock or goth bands such as HIM, My Chemical Romance, Mindless Self Indulgence, and Marilyn Manson. My Chemical Romance's *Helena*, HIM's *The Kiss of Dawn*, and Marilyn Manson's *Putting Holes in Happiness* all showcase the lead singers, who share an aesthetic of long, black hair, heavy black eye makeup, and skin powdered pale white. They appear both feminine and tragic, reflective of the emotional and melancholic nature of their songs and genre.

Dunja Brill, author of *Goth Culture: Gender, Sexuality, and Style*, explains that "the eccentric diversity and representation of gender within the Goth or Gothic subculture, is often described by its participants as open and liberating."[59] However, none of these videos work toward dismantling gender roles through actions which might re-cast gender dynamics or systemic patriarchy.

Outside the goth context, straight cisgender male artists seem willing to parody gender stereotypes, though unwilling to set new standards that refuse to abide by their gendered role. The Strokes video for *The End has No End* shows a young man in various scenes of his life from high school graduation to his first day of work, dressed in a typical business suit. His wife is shown kissing him goodbye, then cleaning the house. The repetitive nature of the editing serves to show the problematic stasis of this gender binary. The video considers the gender norms and limits which have also affected heterosexual men, who are expected to uphold masculine, patriarchal roles. This is echoed by second-wave feminist pioneer Betty Friedan, author of *The Feminine Mystique*, who says that, "Men weren't really the enemy, they were fellow victims, suffering from an outmoded masculine mystique that made them feel unnecessarily inadequate when there were no bears to kill."[60] Friedan not only suggests that cisgender men have yet to establish a modern expression of their maleness, but that the conditions of modernity no longer allow them to meet the antiquated standards of masculinity to which they continue to hold themselves.

Franz Ferdinand's video *Michael* begins with a performance by the band dressed in all black suits. Doppelgängers descend upon them while they play, essentially demonstrating the facility and ubiquity of the performance of masculinity. All the men are identical replicas with blank faces. The robotic uniformity is emphasized when one of the men's arms is pulled and moves the video into a surreal section where parts of the band's bodies double, and the room swirls around in what becomes a nightmarish mechanical montage that ends the video.

These videos make fair attempts to comment upon the limitations of existing structures, but offer no attempt at a solution or alternative.

It is of note that some cisgender female artists also adopt this kind of parodic strategy, as seen in Pink's 2005 video *Stupid Girls*, which shows women making attempts to fulfill stereotypes of beauty or femininity. One woman chokes on the chemicals of her spray tan. When she exits the tanning booth she is an unnatural orange color. Another scene shows Pink as a plastic surgery patient lying on a gurney with markings all over her body where she is to be operated on. Germaine Greer considers the kind of compulsive attempts toward perceived physical perfection dramatized in the video as, "dissatisfaction with the body as it is [...] an insistent desire that it be otherwise, not natural but controlled, fabricated [...] [the] disguise of the actual, arising from fear and distaste."[61] Greer observes beauty less as an expression of vanity than an act towards control, stemming from fear. In contrast, Pink, like the Strokes, fails to offer a solution or interpretation of the constructions of femininity she condemns, and further alienates her subjects as "stupid."

X. PUSSY FEMINISM

Pink's video attempts a comical, less radical, and ultimately less effective approach to feminist representation. Though it seeks to assert that women need not commodify femininity, and critiques the extreme, sometimes dangerous, methods of doing so, its reproduction of toxic stereotypes fails to consider a source of this behavior. I have qualified several other videos that make fairly weak attempts at feminist positioning as representing "Pussy Feminism." The use of the word "pussy" draws on the term's history as a derogatory insult for weakness. Appropriated here in a feminist context, its embedded shock value simply asks for "more" — more intensity, more power, more provocative alternatives. In 2007, for example, Fergie of the band Black Eyed Peas released a video for the song *Big Girls Don't Cry*, which was the fourth best-selling single of the year.[62] Fergie serves as one example of an artist whose visual media fails to push the boundaries extended by their predecessors. Though the song's lyrical themes advise emotional strength with lines like "I've got to get a move on with my life, it's time to be a big girl now,"[63] the imagery of the video is as tame as one might expect from an artist who only aspires to be a "big girl." The imagery of the video implies female agency by showing Fergie leaving her lover, but not until she has assumed the victimhood of having her heart broken by him. She spends most of the video vulnerably displayed in her underwear. The underwear's arguably childlike ruffled edges — a nod to the song's title, perhaps — starkly contrast the sexually provocative and sophisticated couture designs worn by her pop counterparts such as Beyoncé or Lady Gaga.

In a study on the effects of music video on youth culture in 1987, Michael Brake observed that "adolescent females receive distinct signals about the cult of femininity from popular fiction and mass media, and these cues have a central theme: romantic attachment and dependency on men."[64] As exemplified by Fergie, this trend for glamorized feminine imagery dripping with saccharine, yet relatable, sentiments of heartbreak and loneliness continues, despite a revival of controversial media by pop music's female leaders.

The release of Katy Perry's video *I Kissed a Girl* is another example. Perry's appropriation of homosexuality in the song and video stands as an example of the erotic investment flirted with by heterosexuals. Perry makes her same-sex encounter a one-off novelty, and includes no imagery in the video which might contradict the notion of disposability she embeds with lyrics such as, "No, I don't even know your name, it doesn't matter. You're my experimental game, just human nature."[65] Beyoncé's *If I Were a Boy* explores subversion in a similar fantasy-based mode. In this video, Beyoncé plays the role of a police officer. The role will later be adopted by a man to expose her fantasy of having the authority she perceives as specifically male. These videos express an interest in the destabilization of gender roles and sexuality, though those interests are ultimately treated as disposable or implausible.

X. ASSIMILATION

When I began this section it seemed that since the legalization of same sex-marriage in 2003, music video was following the social trend toward gender equality through greater queer and feminist representation in the medium. The view I have of this progression has since become more nuanced and multifaceted. There are extremely few queer artists in the mainstream. Sam Smith, Adam Lambert, and Frank Ocean are perhaps the most prominent male examples, and arguably represent themselves with homonormative imagery, or imagery that obscures the representation of their sexuality altogether. Lisa Duggan's particular definition of homonormativity perhaps best highlights the downfall of such a strategy. Homonormativity, she says, "does not contest dominant heteronormative assumptions and institutions, but upholds and sustains them, while promising the possibility of a demobilized gay constituency and a privatized, depoliticized gay culture anchored in domesticity and consumption."[66] As Duggan suggests, homonormativity fails to claim queer space or express its character and validity. Rather, homonormative representations preserve existing systems and limits by seeking to adapt to them. The rarity and bravery of these men being "Out" as mainstream artists bears its own political significance. Though not exactly "privatized" in that regard they all are, however, fairly a-political in their video work. As previously mentioned, despite recently incorporating small amounts of queer imagery into his work, Ocean makes no overt references to his sexuality in his videos, nor are his videos embedded with any critique of a system in which he kept that sexuality private for so long. Lambert makes his stand with the unabashed expression of his flamboyant persona, though he is typically embedded in heteronormative culture, where said persona is created through rampant consumption of designer goods and cosmetic abundance. Though these two artists might stand to exemplify greater acceptance of queer artists in the mainstream, their video work seems both self-satisfied to have assimilated into popular culture and complacent about advancing that acceptance further through a broader view of a policed system.

That broader view is, however, certainly highlighted by several of the queer artists explored in this section who fall outside the mainstream. Le1f, Peaches, and SSION, for example, use iconography in imagined environments, which makes for an anti-assimilation critique of hetero-sexist systems: Le1f's use of commercial goods in deviant sex acts, Peaches' libidinal lesbian imagery set in a domestic space which must be uncovered, SSION's appropriation of masculine symbols and his departure from, and invasion of policed institutions such as a school and a suburban home. Their sexuality is overt and usually defined by the dynamics of the video, though the narratives never portray typical romances where a couple ultimately comes together or falls apart in the melodramatic tradition of so many heterosexual narratives played out in film and video.

Other artists' critiques of Lady Gaga are also of note for her tenuous alignment with queer culture from within the mainstream. Gaga defies feminine and masculine boundaries supposedly in the name of empowering women and the gay and the queer community, though her significance to that community has been criticized by other queer female artists. Peaches explained the difference between herself and Gaga by saying, "She has television as her outlet, which I don't. I'm not really invited on TV. They don't want me on TV because I'm old, I don't know, I'm weird."[67] Beth Ditto, lesbian frontwoman of the band the Gossip, echoes this. She says, "For my group of friends is Lady Gaga eye-opening? No. She's a less dangerous version of what was so cool about pop culture in the 80s. Back then it was so gay and so punk in so many ways."[68]

Despite the similarities of aesthetics, sound, and message in their work, Peaches reiterates the fact that she has not been assimilated into the mainstream, while Ditto belittles Gaga's work as comparably safe and less controversial than that which preceded it decades before. The fact that these women are in direct competition with Gaga is fair to note as a possible motivation for their harsh critiques, though it affirms that they have not assimilated to her mainstream glorification of gender equality — they have not "bought in," as it were, to her, or the equality she purports to advance and represent. Lady Gaga's attitude and the attitude against her might be further understood through the critique of the Marxist geographer David Harvey, who says that "wonderful-sounding words like 'freedom', 'liberty', 'choice' [...] hide the grim realities of the restoration and reconstruction of naked class power, locally as well as trans-nationally, but most particularly in the main financial centres of global capitalism."[69]

Harvey essentially identifies egalitarian buzzwords as rebranding capitalist practices — a strategy which Gaga could certainly be accused of adopting. Though perhaps transparent to gay artists with whom she also stands in competition, is this not still a more positive capitalist venture than the glut of violent, sexist, homophobic propaganda still unapologetically produced?

As we have seen in the previous section, the mainstream is marked with a few renegades whose work has warranted elaboration for its cinematic value and violent critiques of heterosexist representation. These and other works by queer artists have expanded the vocabulary of gender represented in music video and have reignited an anti-assimilation campaign which leads more by exemplary subversion than by declarative social activism. The relationship of queer representation in the mainstream to a capitalist agenda is a tenuous one, though perhaps an investment worth making if it means devaluing and displacing hetero-sexist norms.

PART THREE

X.

This section undertakes a closer consideration of the cultural context informing a subversive visual. In this regard, these works have produced more specific forms of social activism, whose subversive gender representations are also more acutely responsive to their time. While the proliferation of gender identities explored in the previous section was positioned largely as a post-internet affect, this was not thematically addressed in these artists' work.

We'll examine the first major crisis to which music video had the opportunity to respond, the AIDS crisis, and perhaps the most recent controversy which has inspired a noticeable and exceptional body of work in response, the Black Lives Matter movement. I recognize that since 1981 there have been several cultural crises which these frames do not address — environmental issues and war are perhaps most notable among those absences. However, such crises produced comparably less queer and feminist work in response. Though a comprehensive analysis of cultural events since 1981 cannot be made, this section's approach is necessary to consider how agency is utilized, how artists actively use the medium (as compared to how boundaries of representation have been changed due to shifting modes of distribution and regulation, as previously considered), and how methods of subversion have changed in response to cultural conditions.

X.

The first official report on AIDS was released on 5 June 1981,[1] when The United States Center for Disease Control and Prevention published a morbidity report, which described the same rare lung infection in five young, healthy, gay men in Los Angeles.[2] MTV first aired two months later, on 1 August 1981. The work explored in this section marks the medium's first response to a major cultural crisis. These works navigate multiple facets of that crisis, though their queer and feminist strategies underscore concerns with the representation of gender and sexuality throughout.

These works confronted the reprehensible silence and conservatism of the era. President Ronald Reagan did not engage with AIDS policy and did not publicly say the word "AIDS" until 1987.[3] Reagan's failure to publicly acknowledge AIDS would ultimately be qualified as one of the most significant obstacles to controlling it. In 1987, the surgeon general, Dr C. Everett Koop, produced a report citing education as crucial to fighting the disease. The report emphasized comprehensive sex education in elementary and secondary schools, condom usage, home-based family discussions on sexuality, and monogamy.[4] In addition to the silent handling of the crisis by the president, conservative measures were also taken that actively worked against Koop's assessment that, "Ignorance regarding sexuality in general, and the spread of sexually transmitted diseases in particular, were the most substantial barriers to controlling the disease."[5]

Examples of such conservative barriers included the establishment of the Parents Music Resource Center (PMRC) and the project of defunding the national arts organization, the National Endowment for the Arts (NEA). Both projects were fueled by a desire to censor sexual representation in popular culture and high art respectively. These are arenas that would seem key to disseminating a broader knowledge of sexuality and safe sex practices and to potentially highly diverse audiences. Marjorie Heins describes the era of censorship during the AIDS crisis by saying, "It was tempting to find new demons among any group that challenged the imagined 'traditional values' utopia of our mythical past: sexual non-conformists, provocative artists, pornographers."[6] Heins' quote further reinforces that conservatives likely would have perceived musicians and artists as threats worthy of taking direct action against through the PMRC and the defunding of the NEA.

The supposed mission of the PMRC was to prevent music with explicit content from being sold to minors. However, it was qualified more acutely as "a reactionary form of censorship"[7] by music scholar Claude Chastagner. Similarly, the NEA had been under attack in the late 1980s by Senator Jesse Helms of North Carolina, among other conservatives, for disbursing public funds to organizations that had exhibited work by artists such as Andres Serrano and Robert Mapplethorpe, which Helms considered obscene.[8] Those works included Serrano's image *Piss Christ* (1987), which showed a crucifix submerged in urine, and Mapplethorpe's graphic homoerotic photo series meant to comprise part of the NEA-funded exhibition *Robert Mapplethorpe: The Perfect Moment* at the Corcoran Gallery of Art in 1989 (the show was ultimately cancelled because of the condemnatory conservative response to it).

Silence and conservatism contradict the typical cultural response to crisis, which is to provide awareness and action. This project was ambitiously undertaken by artists such as George Michael, Salt-N-Pepa, and TLC who advocated safe-sex practices and AIDS awareness in their videos.

X.

Though seemingly antithetical to much of the work explored in this book, which uses music video to combat gender norms rather than reinforce them, I am touching briefly on George Michael's video *I Want Your Sex* to exemplify the homophobia that sustained Michael's performance of a hetero-masculine role, and how he used this to impart a message of safe-sex.

Michael reflected on the private fear that informed his decision to conceal his sexuality, saying in an interview that, "In the years when HIV was a killer, any parent of an openly gay person was terrified."[9] Michael connects his sexuality to the fear of death and loss presented by AIDS and HIV. He projects this fear onto his family in defense of his secrecy, as well as "every parent of an openly gay person." He addresses a broader social mentality in relation to his own attempt to protect his family by hiding his sexuality. In addition to signifying a private fear of familial trauma, Michael signifies the unwarranted public fear of the homosexual body as an extension of a fear of AIDS and HIV during this period. Michael evades the hysteria surrounding gay men as a symbol of the disease through his performance of heterosexual norms.

He engages with the sexual politics sparked by AIDS and HIV as his hetero-persona, despite the fact that alignment with the disease was what he supposedly feared about coming out. *I Want Your Sex* opens with a cropped body shot of a woman in a corset. The shot cuts to a woman's face, eyes closed and smiling; then a shot of black satin sheets. The fabric gathers and recedes, implicitly with the movement of bodies — the heterosexual bodies of Michael and his female partner — entwined beneath. More direct is the image that follows. Michael ties a red ribbon over the eyes of the woman. This is, in itself, a subversive sexual act marrying trust and deprivation. These shots illustrate that Michael was not only willing to "dress" the part of a heterosexual man, but willing to "play" the part, representing explicit scenes of sexual activity with the woman. Michael is subsequently shown, also blindfolded, in bed kissing her. Shots of the woman's body being showered in water are then shown, making explicit reference to ejaculation. Michael's body is also shown, showered in water, while the woman's painted red nails rest on his chest. What follows is a moment of sexual advocacy, delivered in a mode still consistent with the hyper-sexual hetero-imitation Michael has staged throughout the video and his career to that point. While in bed with the woman, Michael spells out "Explore" on her thigh in red lipstick, then the word "Monogamy" across her back [Figure 22].

Figure 22: George Michael, *I Want Your Sex*, 1987

The last shot of the video returns to the image scrolled again in lipstick against a white background. This acts as a direct response to promiscuity as a cause of the spread of HIV and AIDS. Though he establishes a concern for sexual health, Michael sacrifices a position as an advocate for safe sex within the gay community, instead pushing the same message through a heteronormative agenda.

Michael would continue to perform this role until his public outing in 1998. Moreover, in addition to highlighting an early response to AIDS in music video and the homophobia of the period, this deliberate and stereo-typical performance of masculinity destabilizes the notion that masculinity and heterosexuality stem from maleness. Butler echoes this in her assertion that, "the naturalistic effects of heterosexualized genders are produced through imitative strategies; what they imitate is a phantasmatic ideal of heterosexual identity, one that is produced by the imitation as its effect."[10]

Butler suggests above that there is no origin from which gender is produced. Rather, the repeated imitation of heterosexualized genders gives the effect of naturalism. Though Michael's masculinity is not a product of his maleness or homosexuality, his imitation of maleness based on what Butler calls a "phantasmatic ideal of heterosexual identity," relies on his conscious performance of masculinity. While the examples in this text are analyzed for the specific meanings of their break from the conventions of gender performance, Michael's performance exposes precisely the learned roles from which the artists in this text break.

I will compare Michael's mode of sexual advocacy in music video with that of the female hip-hop acts Salt-N-Pepa and TLC, who promoted sexual communication and safety in videos such as *Let's Talk About Sex* and *Ain't 2 Proud 2 Beg* respectively. Unlike Michael, neither group pushed monogamous, heterosexual relationships as necessary keys to AIDS prevention. In doing so, they combatted homophobia by exposing the myth that promiscuity is a proclivity specific to gay men, and promoted a feminist message as independent women in control of their sexuality and health. Salt-N-Pepa and TLC aligned themselves directly with the AIDS prevention movement, which was especially crucial given that they represented a community widely affected by the disease, if comparably less stigmatized by it than gay men were. In 1986, the Center for Disease Control reported that the incidence rate of AIDS among black and Hispanic subjects was three times as high as that of white subjects.[11] Author Jonathan Engel also notes that research institutions were growing because the epidemic was growing. He says, "Although new infections among gay men had declined dramatically by 1990, new infections among other high-risk groups had increased even faster."[12] The artists in these two musical groups used their platform from within a highly affected community to raise awareness about AIDS prevention. Their confrontation of sexual issues subverted historically expected sexual modesty from cisgender women. In expressing caution about sex, however, they did not compromise the expression of their sexuality and sexual desire. The result is a feminist self-possession underscored by messages of sexual responsibility and social awareness.

Salt-N-Pepa's *Let's Talk About Sex* video opens with a shot from within a trashcan, showing a book labeled "Talk Sex" being discarded. The group's members are smiling, spliced with shots of male dancers. The shot of the women giggling acknowledges the difficulty of discussing the taboo subject matter, but marks that discussion necessary by their continuation. We are returned to the shot from within the trashcan, where we see a child retrieve the discarded sex book. This suggests that sex should not be a strictly "adult" topic — that sexual education is crucial to youth. The child flips through pages, revealing for the camera that "Sex" is the only word in the book, printed on every page, declaring it the inescapable topic of the video. This is juxtaposed with an image of an adult man, presumably a radio DJ, indicated by the lit-up "ON AIR" sign on the desk in front of him. The DJ has been bound and gagged, symbolizing the commercial music industry's reluctance to address sexual issues. In a subsequent scene we see that group member Salt has taken over the DJ's position at the "ON AIR" microphone.

This scene is of note for its critique of systemic practices and hierarchies, namely those of the PMRC. Salt takes over the male DJ's position of authority, initiating the sexual dialogue with which the DJ was reluctant to engage.

The scenes of dancing continue, showing us sexualized, free bodies. As the refrain consistently reminds us to "talk about sex," however, sexual expression is anchored to the responsibility to communicate. The group adopts various costumes throughout, which stretch the economy of femininity and the expectations of the female gender. They portray construction workers and catcall at male passers-by, symbolizing a penetration of a typically male profession and the public expression of their sexual desire. In another scene, the group's DJ, Spinderalla, walks by a seated row of men. She wears a skin-tight white dress and inserts herself in between two of them, wrapping her arms around them in an act of fraternal inclusion. The shot of the group from the beginning wearing black evening apparel with styled hair is juxtaposed with a shot of them wearing baggy jeans and oversized men's shirts and jackets. The effect is one observed by Suzanne Bost in her discussion of similar female hip-hop artist, Da Brat:

Da Brat's covert critique is internal to Hip Hop marketing. She molds her image to be recognizable within the stereotypical gender codes of an exhibitionist "ho" and a gun-toting "gangsta;" but by fusing the two in one body, she deconstructs the binary assumed to be at their foundation. Each pole is undermined as a result: a whore cannot be a whore or an object of others' sexual mastery, if she is also a pimp and a gangster.[13]

Throughout the video, Salt-N-Pepa are, as Bost describes Da Brat to be, sexy, feminine, masculine, and able to transgress the social boundaries that these aesthetics often signify. These images challenge gender norms, while still laced with a sense of fun and energy. They lead up to the insertion of a subversive memento mori, reminding their audience of consequences of sexual irresponsibility. A fake skeleton is shown with a large, round sign outlined in red that reads: "AIDS." Over the skeleton's mouth is yellow police-style tape with the word "censored" [Figure 23]. The image reiterates the AIDS slogan, "Silence Equals Death." It suggests that censoring our dialogue about sex will act in direct contribution to AIDS-related deaths by failing to provide knowledge about its prevention. In addition to advocating through the video, the group also released an alternate version of the song available on promotional radio singles, and some B-sides of the single re-titled "Let's Talk About AIDS." In this version of the track, Salt-N-Pepa remind their listeners that AIDS is unrelated to race and sexuality. They outline various modes of transmission and correct false information about the spread of the disease.

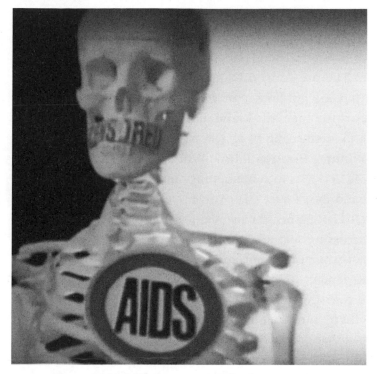

Figure 23: Salt-N-Pepa, *Let's Talk About Sex*, 1991

With *Let's Talk About Sex,* Salt-N-Pepa made subversive attacks on traditional feminine norms by adopting both masculine and feminine dress and addressing explicit subject matter. They advised social awareness, while also making political jabs at the institutions (radio and the PMRC) who submitted to and promoted censorship of such topics during a period when their discussion was of crucial importance.

TLC took a similarly aggressive approach to safe sex awareness by subverting feminine norms in their video

Ain't 2 Proud 2 Beg. Though the title would imply a sense of inferiority by not being "too proud," the video suggests sexual consumption, rather than availability and submission. The implication here is not that the members of TLC are concerned about whether they are desired. They are not hoping or waiting to be chosen as partners, as is the thematic foundation of pop songs employed by a diverse scope of artists, ranging from R'n'B legend, Whitney Houston ("How Will I Know if he Really Loves Me" (1985)) to contemporary female-fronted garage rock band Best Coast ("Do You Love Me Like You Used To?" (2012)). Rather, the members of TLC express concern about accessing sex, not love. In the video, several men offer gift-wrapped presents to TLC member Lisa "Left Eye" Lopes, Rozonda "Chilli" Thomas, and Tionne "T-Boz" Watkins, as if courting them. The girls roll their eyes, and reject the gifts by throwing them to the background of the shot. The fact that they are not too proud to beg is a bold declaration of their sexual desire, not their desire to be a committed partner. This is expressed throughout the video, yet responsibly set alongside visual references to safe sex.

Similar to George Michael's useage of words written in lipstick to deliver an anti-promiscuity message to his audience, TLC use graffiti-style script presented on screen for sexual expression and advice. "I wanna be touched" is the first message of the video, followed by the song's title. The words "Safe Sex" then move across the white background.

Another way that TLC advocated safe sex was by turning condoms into fashion accessories. Left Eye wears a condom as an eye patch [Figure 24] and pinned on to her clothes.

She appropriates the contraception typically aligned with maleness and discretion or privacy. The act declares her responsibility for her own sexual health and suggests that condoms are not only necessary, but — given the mainstream popularity of the group — cool and fashionable.

Figure 24: TLC, *Ain't 2 Proud 2 Beg*, 1992

Unlike Salt-N-Pepa, TLC never default to feminine dress in this video. Despite their masculine presentation, however, the girls use a male figure as a kind of prop to reinforce their heterosexual desire. The male figure is shown shirtless, sweaty, and flexing his muscles. In a shot of his backside, the girls approach him and pull his jeans down to reveal a large X on white underwear, indicating his lower half as a veritable target ("'X' marks the spot"). The girls have effectively subverted traditional female appearance and courting norms, while objectifying male subjects, and declaring their desire for safe sex, which they also advocate to their audience.

X.

The works included below explore the intersection of black sexual and racial identity in dialogue with the Black Lives Matter movement, which began in 2012. Some of these works overtly reference the organization, while others' queer and feminist imagery represent the movement's mission toward greater visibility, acceptance, and the protection of all black bodies — specifically those further marginalized by gender and sexuality. This section also returns to the dramatic theory of Bertolt Brecht as a means of considering how these performances are further complicated and actualized through their relationship with their audience.

While it is regrettable that this chapter does not cover works by artists of more varied races and cultures, this was not a choice that reflects any idea that the Black Lives Matter movement might preclude support of other subjugated racial groups. Rather, this absence is symptomatic of a comparable lack of work made in this time frame by, for example, Hispanic or Asian artists, which I might qualify as having elements of gender subversion worth exploring at length. The video work of Uruguay's Dani Umpi, though rich with surreal characters and queer iconography, is an extension of his main focus — his visual and performance art practice. As such, his videos might be better placed in dialogue with the oeuvres of similar visual artists who also work with music video, such as Andrew Thomas Huang, or visual artists that maintain a performance practice, such as Kembra Pfahler (The Voluptuous Horror of Karen Black). Other queer, non-black, artists of color incorporating subversive gender imagery include Brazil's Rico Dalasam, Mexico's Zemmoa, and Spain's La Prohibida. However, rather than attempt to tie these few artists into a discourse embedded in American history and politics, where — unlike the Central and South American countries the artists I have mentioned hail from — people of color are the more intensely marginalized, I have chosen to narrow my focus for a more concentrated analysis. Preferably, given a wider array of subversive work, this chapter could have taken a more global perspective of the intersectionality of race, sexuality, and culture. The noticeable lack of queer work by artists of a broader range of races and cultures is echoed by Doris Leibetseder, who has also focused on queer modes of subversion in music. In her book *Queer Tracks: Subversive Strategies in Rock and Pop Music*, she notes,

One difficulty that I did not manage to overcome to my satisfaction was to find queer musicians of various racial, ethnic, or religious backgrounds [...] I came across the hip-hop bands of colour, Yo! Majesty and The Lost Bois and whilst I was finishing the conclusion, I found the names Miz Korona, Mz Jonz, Thee Satisfaction, Las Krudas, Skim, Collin Clay, Big Freedia, and Karlyn Heffernan.[14]

I have included this passage to confirm a shared frustration among scholars for a lack of diversity in popular music, though I find similar inadequacy in Leibetseder's mention of these contemporary queer, black, hip-hop artists without any analysis of their work. My own decision to exclude some of the artists she mentions in this section is due to their lack of subversive gender imagery in their videos specifically. This is the same reason for the absence of further discussion of videos by the very few queer Asian artists I found, such as Japan's Ki Yo and Hong Kong's Chet Lam and Enno Cheng. I would also like to clarify that some works by black artists, which are certainly of note for their queer and feminist merits, such as the Grace Jones' video *I'm Not Perfect, But I'm Perfect for You*, directed by Keith Haring, RuPaul's *Back to My Roots* and *A Shade Shady*, or Lil Kim's *Crush on You*, have been excluded in prioritization of examining works made in response to this contemporary social moment.

The works in this chapter bring us to question the multi-faceted complexities faced by their subjects: Why am I not an American if I am black? Why am I not black if I am queer? Defiant of a history of erasure, these videos show black, queer, and feminist bodies, affirming their struggle and their existence. In some of these works, the very proclamations of blackness are of note for their rare enunciation in popular music. These tracks' and videos' expression of pride in, and ownership of, blackness adds an element which is at once exclusionary to white audiences (a contradiction to the perception of popular media as being accessible and inclusionary), yet vital to the project of black visibility and affirmation. We are brought to question how different meanings are created amongst audiences of different races, and also how that same exclusionary element may simply go unquestioned when white artists fail to make music with which people of color may identify. However, while these videos may work towards a correction of the lack of representation inherent in the continued marginalization of these groups, we will also consider how authentic those representations are and whether they also represent the artist or simply the artist's desire to participate in the growth and veneration of Black Lives Matter. Because the privileged position of some of the artists we will discuss starkly contrasts with the lower cultural status of the subjects in their videos, and the majority of the audiences watching them (regardless of race), these videos are not without certain tensions that bear addressing across existing black studies discourse.

Before I elaborate on some specific questions of this section, I would like to establish that this chapter is not meant to explore the precarity of dueling identities: whether a subject may privilege, for example, their black identity over their queer identity or vice versa. It is also not my intention to locate blackness as a source of subversion, but to consider how it further complicates the gender issues we have hitherto explored, and how Black Lives Matter may have inspired more provocative and explicit enunciations of gendered blackness in recent video work. This chapter also does not seek to compare and contrast queer and feminist representations by artists of color with those made by white artists, which would perpetuate the kind of binary thinking inherent in racism, sexism, and heterosexism. Due to the aforementioned ties of this section to

Black Lives Matter, I will begin with a brief review of the movement.

Drawing inspiration from the American Civil Rights and Black Power movements of the 1960s, Black Lives Matter was created in 2012 by Alicia Garza, Patrisse Cullors, and Opal Tometi in response to the acquittal of neighborhood watch volunteer, George Zimmerman, for the shooting of the unarmed, black, seventeen-year-old Trayvon Martin in Sanford, Florida. The movement gained global support and recognition following two similar cases where black, unarmed suspects were killed by members of law enforcement who were not indicted: the 2014 shooting of eighteen-year-old Michael Brown in Ferguson, Missouri, and the suffocation of forty-three-year-old Eric Garner in Staten Island, New York, also in 2014. These cases produced slogans and symbols which were employed in protest by activist groups and are of note for the allusions made to them in popular music and music video. For example, because Michael Brown was believed to have put his hands up in surrender to his killer, protesters across the country employed the chant "Hands Up, Don't Shoot," and gathered in groups with their arms raised, mirroring Brown's alleged pose of surrender.[15] Beyoncé referenced this in her track "7/11," repeating, "My hands up, my hands up. Flexin' while my hands up. My hands up, my hands up. I stand up with my hands up." By adding to the phrase that she is standing up, and "flexin" — as in standing up for herself, and flexing her muscles — she brings a power to the phrase historically aligned with surrender and contextually representative of systemic violence. She is simultaneously protesting the death of Brown through the phrase, while asserting strength and unity, rather than victimhood. In Beyoncé's *Formation* video, which we will explore in greater depth later in this section, a young black boy dances in front of a long row of riot police. They eventually raise their hands, symbolizing the "Hands up. Don't shoot." slogan associated with the shooting of Brown. The camera proceeds to pan across a wall spray-painted with the words "Stop shooting us," directly implicating the police as targeting young, unarmed, black subjects. In "Feedback," Kanye West incorporates the reference with a more direct accusation of police; he sings, "Hands up, we just doing what the cops taught us. Hands up, hands up, then the cops shot us."

In the case of Eric Garner, his final words, "I can't breathe," repeated eleven times as shown in a video taken by bystander Ramsey Orta, have been directly quoted or referenced by artists to protest his death and reflect Black Lives Matter more broadly. In Rhianna's "American Oxygen," she sings, "Breathe out, breathe in, American Oxygen. Every breath I breathe, chasin' the American dream." With these lyrics, she invokes the idea of air, breath, and life as tied to the freedom, justice, and ambition synonymous with "the American dream." By this logic, when Garner "can't breathe" his liberties have been compromised and we must question why. Spliced with sections of Rhianna singing in front of a waving American flag, the song's video is largely comprised of footage of significant moments of black resistance and black achievement: scenes from the riots that ensued in Ferguson after Brown's death; Barack Obama, the first American President of color, taking the oath of office; and track stars John Carlos and Tommie Smith giving the Black Power salute during their medal ceremony at the 1968 Olympics in Mexico City. While celebrating black Americans, the video also suggests the difficulty of being recognized *as* American as a person of color — of being given the same rights and liberties as white Americans, which draws us back to the racism to which Garner was subjected. In addition to these examples by Beyoncé, West, and Rhianna, the abundance of work produced in direct response to Black Lives Matter was tracked by a now defunct website, Sounds of BLM. At the time of writing it had cited one-hundred-and-five musical tracks, and thirty-two videos by a diverse group of artists ranging from Russian, queer, feminist, punk band Pussy Riot to black, American, male, rappers such as Kendrick Lamar and Yasiin Bey (formerly Mos Def).

Since the deaths of Brown and Garner, attention has been brought to dozens of other cases of police brutality and institutionalized violence against unarmed black subjects. Before turning to focus upon some of the videos whose compelling images and complicated symbols warrant further analysis, it is worth clarifying that this chapter's focus on Black Lives Matter bears particular relevance to this book for the movement's queer politics. In addition to its mission of combatting racism, Black Lives Matter makes a point of expressing equal attention to its queer faction. In a statement from their official website posted at the time of writing, they asserted,

Black Lives Matter affirms the lives of Black queer and trans folks, disabled folks, Black-undocumented folks, folks with records, women and all Black lives along the gender spectrum [...] It is a tactic to (re)build the Black liberation movement.[16]

The above statement reinforces that Black Lives Matter is, in itself, a queer movement, and a movement for other marginalized groups. The queer consciousness of Black Lives Matter should be considered a distinct element of artists' message when they invoke the dogma of the movement through their videos. Videos about Black Lives Matter are inherently imbricated in a queer politics. Conversely, whilst queer artists of color such as Le1f and Mykki Blanco may not directly reference Black Lives Matter in their videos, they fundamentally echo the movement's affirmation of queer, black bodies, and the value of their representation. In the following section I would like to consider some of these videos which posit blackness as an integral part of their feminism and queerness.

X.

On Solange Knowles' album *A Seat at the Table*, the track "Don't Touch My Hair" confronts the invasion of her person, blackness, and womanhood by those ignorant to difference. The video begins with slow motion footage of Solange, shaking her head, as her braided and beaded hair moves around her neck and shoulders. In a subsequent shot from overhead, Solange sings up into the camera surrounded by black couples and small groups, who touch through minimal choreography [Figure 25]. Our attention is drawn to the beauty of black bodies in motion, whose subliminal rhythms suggest connection and shared experience.

Figure 25: Solange, *Don't Touch My Hair*, 2016

The music lifts slightly in energy as Solange brings in more direct lines like, "You know this hair is my shit / Rode the ride, I gave it time / But this here is mine." The lines express a possession and defense of black physicality well described by Natalegé Whaley, who says that, "Hair is used as a metaphor for our entire essence on ["Don't Touch My Hair"] and is the perfect symbol, as our hair is one thing that has always been <u>policed throughout history</u> and into the present."[17] The black femininity Whaley refers to is highlighted by Solange in a series of tableaus that defy stereotypes of black women in music video. Women with afros peel vegetables in white slips, seemingly indifferent to being filmed. These images operate in contrast to the history of gross objectification of the black female body, as highlighed in examples ranging from Dr. Dre's *Ain't Nothin' but a "G" Thang* in 1992, or Nelly's *Tip Drill* in 2000, to Young Thug's *Turn Up*, released in 2016. She surrounds herself with black women, who turn their backs away from the camera. They are not sexualized, nor do they appease, or even meet the gaze of the viewer. Likely referencing her lyric, "Don't touch my crown," Solange stands at the edge of a church pew, with her hair braided into a crown-like shape atop her head. Five black women stand behind the pew, some with hair in a similar style, though all of the women wear highly geometric, ruffled, electric blue, avant-garde costumes. These images' focus on black womanhood is one that bell hooks laments is often subsumed by other sexed and raced categories who receive greater visibility. In *Ain't I a Woman: Black Women in Feminism*, hooks addresses the precarious social position of subjects such as those portrayed in *Don't Touch My Hair.* She claims that, "No other group in America has so had their identity socialized out of existence as have black women.

We are rarely recognized as a group separate and distinct from black men, or as a present part of the larger group 'women' in this culture."[18]

Since the publication of hooks' text, more nuanced identity politics have emerged, which stand to complicate hooks' overriding thesis: how do queer and trans subjects further highlight the narrow scope of our social awareness to womanhood? Who else remains "socialized out of existence?" While this attention to subjectivities within gender categories ultimately strives for a unifying, equalizing politics, Solange corrects what hooks implies to be the historical white-washing of the female experience, by devoting space to the representation of black cis-women. Solange also asserts the critical boundaries she must set in protection of her dignity and to demand respect: Don't touch her hair or treat her as an objectified other. In the track she also says not to touch the pride, glory, or feelings that *are* her hair, which *is* her blackness, which is not removable from her womanhood or feminism.

Julianne Escobedo Shepherd wrote for *Pitchfork* that the track addresses "the way black women are devalued, and meets that with resistance,"[19] and calls Solange's voice "a palliative for the pain she describes, as she names truths to divest them of their power."[20] The video for the track resists the devaluation of black women noted by Escobedo Shepherd by celebrating black physicality, femininity, and connection. In addition to naming painful truths to divest them of power, she also uses video to powerfully fortify images of feminine black womanhood.

X.

Zebra Katz gained international attention when his single, "Ima Read" was used in fashion designer Rick Owens' autumn runway show at Paris Fashion Week in 2012. The track alludes to *Paris is Burning*, a film in which "reading," "shading," and "Voguing" are used as queer performative and competitive strategies. Created on the streets of Harlem in the 1980s, "reading" was, and still is, used to literally read a person by highlighting, often with exaggeration, their flaws: their mannerisms, makeup, clothes, their walk, their accent.[21]

Several black queer rappers have invoked references to *Paris is Burning*, though I'm wary of dwelling on this connection at the risk of obscuring the analysis of these artists in specifically musical terms. In addition to the example of Katz's *Ima Read*, Le1f has incorporated Voguing in live performances and in music videos such as *Koi, Wut*, and *Soda*. In his track "Boom," Le1f welcomes the listener to "Banjee Burger," a play on the "Banjee" stereotype, and the "Banjee Girl Realness" competition in *Paris is Burning*. In the film, "Banjee" is qualified by one of the judges as "Looking like the boy that robbed you a few minutes before you came to Paris' ball."

Rapper Cakes da Killa draws on similar modes of ball culture's glamor and drag in videos such as *Truth Tella*. This black-and-white video recalls vintage Hollywood headshots, as Cakes da Killa models a series of extravagant hats [Figure 26]. He also directly notes his relationship to the film in an interview with music website *THUMP*, saying, "Like many butch queens, ballroom swag has had a huge influence on my musicality and confidence [...] I have *Paris Is Burning* to thank for my introduction to the culture."[22]

Figure 26: Cakes da Killa, *Truth Tella*, 2014

Despite confirming the film's influence and importance to his work, his references to ball culture are by no means overly identifiable or consistent . For example, the video *Talkin Greezy* takes place in unglamorous, unpretentious New York City locales — a run-down apartment, Brooklyn stoops, a dominos match in the park, a barber shop — and sees Cakes shed the feminine aesthetics he dons in *Truth Tella* and *Goodie Goodies* for casual, masculine, athletic gear and a masculine gold grill. Azealia Banks makes frequent references to Voguing and Banjee girls, as in the tracks "Fierce" and "Van Vogue," though neither her video work nor her general image rely on the aesthetics of ball culture.

Any suggestion that contemporary queer hip-hop has effectively been sourced from *Paris is Burning*, as has been claimed by scholars such as Stan Hawkins,[23] stands to limit the discourse around these artists. Comparing these artists to subjects in *Paris is Burning* removes them from contemporary hip-hop discourse, drawing them back in time, rather than considering how they might impact or be affected by the present. By comparison, I've looked at Mykki Blanco and Le1f alongside their contemporaries SSION and Frank Ocean, among others.

Another way that such a comparison is limiting is in the precarious relationship it draws between these artists, and the imitative and appropriative strategies adopted by the subjects of *Paris is Burning*. In the film, drag contestants rely on imitation and appropriation of commercial feminine aesthetics to make them feel secure — secure in their feminine identity, but also, literally, physically safe. In the film there are competitions for "realness," which drag queen and ball hostess Dorian Corey calls the ability to pass as a "real woman," or to closet their homosexuality so effectively that, as Corey elaborates in the film,

> They're undetectable. When they can walk out of that ballroom, and into the sunlight, and onto the subway and get home and still have all their clothes and no blood running off their bodies, those are the femme realness queens.[24]

As this quote highlights, for many of the subjects in *Paris is Burning*, drag was a system of survival predicated on constructed norms of femininity, and specifically *white* femininity. This is further echoed by bell hooks, who notes that,

> For black males to take appearing in drag seriously, be they gay or straight, is to oppose a hetero-sexist representation of black manhood [...] Yet the subversive power of those images is radically altered when informed by a racialized fictional construction of the "feminine" that suddenly makes the representation of whiteness as crucial to the experience of female impersonation as gender, that is to say when the idealized notion of the female/feminine is really a sexist idealization of white womanhood. This is brutally evident in Jennie Livingstone's new film, *Paris is Burning*.[25]

When authors such as Hawkins claim that contemporary queer hip-hop artists have "extended the aesthetics and ideologies of ball culture,"[26] I think he fails to consider hooks' argument and he ultimately deflects white imitation and appropriation onto these artists. However, I do not believe that hooks' proposal negates some of the positive aspects of ball culture to which, I think, Hawkins does allude: community, support, collaboration, creativity, and the ability of marginalized queer and black subjects to make power marked by status and beauty — however contentious those qualifiers are — their own. The point here is that while the references made to *Paris in Burning* are noteworthy, they do not constitute the basis for these artists' work, nor does a discourse focused on establishing that foundation service an accurate reading of the broader landscape of contemporary hip-hop. In an interview with *Village Voice*, Le1f references an article for *Pitchfork*, and echoes the disproportionate focus paid in the article to Le1f's relationship to ball culture. Le1f says of the article, "I didn't think there was enough of a distinction between what was going on in terms of our musical scene and the ballroom/Voguing scene. There are ties and references and things [...] but it's not as though I'm going to balls, and my music is not at the ballrooms."[27]

In the same interview, Le1f notably mentions his dance background and that his interest in Voguing is shared with other dance forms such as Butoh and movement incorporated in Fluxus. Among other musical influences, Le1f notably highlights other contemporary hip-hop artists A$AP Rocky, Mykki Blanco, and Lakutis, clearly in an effort to draw his work into dialogue with the contemporary music scene.[28] Unlike the subjects of *Paris is Burning*, whose balls are, as house mother Pepper Lebeija explains, "more or less our fantasy of being a superstar — like the Oscars, or being on the runway as a model"[29] — which have historically largely featured white women — Cakes da Killa and Zebra Katz have, by comparison, cited black female musicians such as Lil Kim[30] and Grace Jones[31] as significant influences.

I have delved into the connection between these artists' works and *Paris is Burning* in order to consider and question the aspects of imitation and appropriation of white culture with which this alignment is weighted. Though some of these artists do include Voguing and references to ball culture, others such as Blanco neither hail from this culture nor reference it in their work. Exploring this relationship also serves to highlight a significant shift between Zebra

Katz's *Ima Read* in 2012 and his work produced after the inception of Black Lives Matter: *1Bad B*tch* and *Blk Diamond*.

Unlike *Ima Read*, these videos do not seek to appropriate white privilege, but rather directly attack it. In *1 Bad B*tch*, Katz arrives at grand white mansion with two white women dressed in nurse uniforms. An elderly white woman answers the door, wearing jewelry and a feather boa, signifying her wealth. Katz's white female accomplices seem to establish that it is not white women that he targets, but rather the white supremacy and privilege signified by the array of bleached, overwrought commodities that comprise the older woman's superfluous reality. Katz is lead to a dining room, where four additional white women in opulent dresses are seated. One by one, they are escorted upstairs by Katz and the nurse characters. The video concludes with a tableau of Katz seated atop a stuffed polar bear. He is flanked by the women, whose frozen position suggests that they have also been made into stuffed relics. This is confirmed as the shot zooms out, barely revealing that they are within an exhibit at a natural history museum, as exposed by the adjoining cases of displayed taxidermy. This video confronts the negative aspects of the kind of appropriative and imitative practices explored in *Paris is Burning*. The wealthy, white, and glamorous are treated as a problem rather than a paradigm, and thus exposed as a false standard of beauty, femininity, and importance.

In *Blk Diamond*, Katz targets systemic oppression by a white, homophobic patriarchy. The main imagery of the video, which Katz has called "imagery of cruelty,"[32] focuses on the abuse of Katz by two obese white males. Dressed in only black underwear, the men haul Katz by a rope tied around his ankles through a meadow of tall grass and dirt. He is dressed in all black, with a leather harness across his chest and a face mask embellished with diamonds. We see Katz hung upside down, flanked by the two men in a shot hauntingly suggestive of a lynching.[33] One man signals to the other, and a plug is pulled from the core of Katz's body. Metallic liquid begins to pour out and drip down onto Katz's face, suggesting ejaculation. Katz echoes this in the lyrics singing, "Like a black diamond under pressure, loaded up, be my refresher [...] I'm dark and nutritious, high in protein, and I'm so delicious." Katz literally oozes his black queer sexuality. We are encouraged to locate this identity as the target of his enemies — stereotypes of homophobic, old, white men, who signify a history of institutionalized racism, from slavery to the policies of Donald Trump. The men proceed to drill a large black rock, while laughing maniacally. The scene is intercut with footage of Katz in an anguished stagger, spot-lit at night, suggesting the unwanted penetration of the "black diamond" Katz has identified himself as.

In these videos, Zebra Katz explores highly aestheticized images of queer blackness. His identity is further situated through his dramatized abuse by white male oppressors. While other videos in this chapter celebrate queer and feminist blackness, as Katz's do as well, these works boldly propose how black queer identity has been shaped by those that would seek to ignore, destroy, or change it.

In his foundational black studies text *The Souls of Black Folk*, W.E.B. Du Bois explores the idea of a "double-consciousness," where black men are given "no true self-consciousness," but rather, view themselves through the eyes of others.[34] He asserts that black subjectivity is formed through black subjects' relationship to a white society, which, at the time of Du Bois' writing (1903) would have been that of a superior class, resulting in a perpetual sense of inferiority for the black subject Du Bois discusses. In *Blk Diamond*, Katz's queer blackness is highlighted by his relationship to white male villains. He dramatizes his double-consciousness by forcing us to view him through the lens of the homophobic, racist, figures he stereotypes in the video.

This video brings to mind bell hooks' analysis of the Spike Lee film *Do the Right Thing*, in which she says that, "White audiences may enjoy this film because they watch it the same way they approach many television shows with black characters, searching for reassurance that they need not fear that black folks will infringe on their turf." In this passage, hooks suggests that through distance from blackness, white viewers derive a sense of safety. Katz's work reminds us of the systemic violence of racism and white privilege that corrects any notion that white cultural space or history is, or ever has been, even vaguely unthreatening.

X.

I have chosen to conclude with a more concentrated analysis of Beyoncé's 2016 video *Formation*. The video sparked unprecedented controversy and national dialogue for its direct references to Black Lives Matter and the myriad of subversive black, queer, feminist elements, which reinforced the inclusionary project of the movement. Moreover, unlike much of Beyoncé's past work, blackness is acknowledged here at a conscious and confrontational level, seemingly motivated by the cultural climate in which it was produced.

Beyoncé simultaneously released the track and video for "Formation," the first single from her *Lemonade* album, on 6 February 2016. This was one day after Trayvon Martin's birthday, and one day before she performed the song at the halftime show of Super Bowl 50. This strategy drew attention to Martin's death, to Black Lives Matter, and to the fiftieth anniversary of the formation of the Black Panthers, which she noted by dressing herself and her army of female backup dancers in the Panthers' signature militant leather jackets and black berets [Figures 27, 28] during her halftime performance. It also banked on the track being a literal overnight success. It meant Beyoncé was ready to confront any backlash or criticism (which did, in fact, ensue) for the racially-driven themes of the work head on, at an event that stood, not only as a paradigm of white, hetero-sexist masculinity, but one which is typically the most-watched broadcast on television every year in the United States. In this instance, the event garnered the third largest audience in American television history, with a reported 111.9 million viewers.[35]

Figure 27: Black Panther rally, DeFremery Park, Oakland, California, 1968

Figure 28: Beyoncé, Super Bowl 50, Halftime Performance, 2016

While the star's draw was undoubtedly a factor in the increased viewership, the majority of the audience still would have been comprised of the aforementioned white, male faction, according to the recent trends reported by the leading television ratings authority, Nielsen Soundscan.[36] To infiltrate a territory where her obligation to delight and entertain was confounded by a message that would implicate the majority of the audience as complicit in the institutionalized racism protested against by Black Lives Matter was a particularly powerful act of subversion for a black woman, regardless of her level of fame. Even within a black historical context, the ostensible feminization and implied *feminist*ization of the Black Panther uniform also subverted the historically masculine face of the movement. Speaking to an audience that grossly outnumbered her demographically, she spoke for those historically least seen and least heard — a combative representation of black women, black power, and a protest against the continued injustices made against black lives by law enforcement in America.

Like this performance, the feminist subversion inherent in the *Formation* video lies in Beyoncé using her platform within a commercial landscape created and dominated by white men to call for the rise and defense of black lives, and specifically black women: "OK, Ladies, now let's get in formation (information),"[37] she sings in the chorus. By performing feminist identities representative of a scope of classes and cultures, and including queer performers and imagery, Beyoncé validates and elevates black culture and queer and feminist black bodies through a rarely-achieved level of mainstream visibility. This will be reiterated throughout this chapter, so I want to be clear that by this I do not mean that said culture is of low value, nor that she increases the inherent value of that culture. Rather, by increasing the visibility of black culture — an act reflective of her own valuation of it — it is likely that this valuation would be raised for those whose valuation of her is also high. We will explore below the identities she performs throughout the video, and how she attempts to actualize the themes of unity and solidarity expressed by the track.

The video begins with scenes of houses almost entirely submerged in water — a post-Hurricane Katrina representation of New Orleans, Louisiana. An audio clip comes in to support the imagery and set the intention of the song before the music begins. We are asked, "What happened at the New Wildins [New Orleans]?"[38] The rhetorical question recalls the devastation of the natural disaster, which was worsened by the inadequacy of the government's response. The government's negligence, moreover, was widely speculated to have been due to New Orleans' high population of African-Americans (over 60%). New Orleans City Councilman Oliver Thomas commented, "People are too afraid of black people to go in and save them."[39] The Reverend Jesse Jackson asserted that race was, "at least a factor" in the slow response, and added that "[Americans] have an amazing tolerance for black pain."[40]

The clip's raspy southern drawl belongs to Messy Mya (Anthony Barre), a YouTube personality from New Orleans who was murdered in 2010 at the age of twenty-two. Though there is debate about Mya's sexuality, his involvement in the New Orleans' Bounce music community has aligned him with the queer culture celebrated by the genre's musicians. One of Bounce's most prominent figures also featured on the "Formation" track is queer artist Big Freedia, who spoke at Mya's wake. Messy Mya and Big Freedia seem to represent the marginalization of their city and return our attention to a country that would ignore such subjects in the wake of disaster. The inclusion of these queer, underground artists also affirms that Beyoncé's feminist representation is not limited to cis-women. In regard to *Formation*, Dr Zandria F. Roberts asserts that, "At [Beyoncé's] limits, the voices and presence of gender-queer folks enter to take over."[41] Roberts suggests that while Beyoncé may not self-identify as queer, she invokes a queer politics by incorporating artists who broaden the representational scope of a work that asserts the rights and equality of all black lives. She represents black queerness, though through her inclusion of queer artists she does so without falsely claiming the lived experience of a queer person of color.

Despite their bold inclusion on the track, it is worth questioning why Mya and Freedia did not appear in the *Formation* video. Why are they not physically represented, shown, included? However, when the visual album for *Lemonade* was released, other collaborators such as Jack White, the Weeknd, and Kendrick Lamar — male artists of considerably higher profiles than Mya and Freedia, which may have contributed to increased attention to the record — were also absent from the videos for their respective tracks. When asked whether Big Freedia was approached about being in the *Formation* video, Freedia's manager Reid Martin responded via email that, "Beyoncé asked Freedia to participate on the track only a couple days before it was released. Unfortunately, there was no time for Freedia to be included in the actual video."[42] Due to the short time span between completion and release of the song, it would seem that Freedia's vocal was most likely conceived of as an addition to the track as the video was in the latter stages of editing, ultimately making her absence a logistical consequence, rather than tactical decision.

The intention Beyoncé sets out through the inclusion of Mya's question, however, is to probe injustice. Regardless of whether you are Messy Mya or Beyoncé Knowles, you can demand answers. Beyoncé proceeds to establish a line of interrogation into the prejudicial injustices exposed through *Formation*'s visual allusions to Hurricane Katrina and the city of New Orleans. The initial shots of the video contrast flashing lights of a police vehicle with flashing lights worn as a decorative mouthpiece by a young black man at a party. The back of a black, shirtless man dancing with his hands pressed behind him in a prayer pose is shown before the back of a jacket reading "POLICE." A scene showing black teens dancing in a living room is intercut with shots of more flooded homes, New Orleans freeway underpasses, and a minister at a pulpit giving a confrontational look into the camera. It is of note that these, and several other background images of New Orleans, were taken from Abteen Bagheri's 2013 documentary *That B.E.A.T.* Despite covering the New Orleans Bounce genre as a whole, the film is comprised largely of footage featuring young, gay, black men dancing to a genre dubbed in the film "Sissy Bounce" for its queer contingent. The dance halls in which they compete are reminiscent of those featured in *Paris is Burning* — minimal, multi-use performance spaces with the kind of outdated interiors that speak to a scant operational budget of its owner, those that rent it, or both. Over the course of these first few clips of *Formation*, tensions are established between authorities and young, black, many presumably queer, civilians, between the identities we can adopt in private and those we must adopt in public to avoid the threat of punishment, or even death, and between poor black communities, and the America that would watch them drown in flooded waters. By bringing these tensions to light, Beyoncé also calls for their resolution. Her subsequent performances of black feminist identities defy the forces that would seek to ignore or harm such subjects.

Before proceeding to explore this strategy, it is worth considering that, while it is precisely her success which makes Beyoncé a valuable figure to bring attention to these tensions, it could also be argued that her extreme wealth and status compromise her ability — perhaps even her right — to represent marginalized black subjects such as those she exposes and entrenches herself amongst in scenes of New Orleans. There is a marginalization inherent in speaking for others, because it presumes that others cannot speak for themselves. I would like to address two factors which seem to preclude Beyoncé from occupying this position of condescension in this video. First, Beyoncé returns attention to the aftermath of Hurricane Katrina eleven years after it occurred. By putting this event in conversation with the contemporary Black Lives Matter movement, and thus comparable instances of systemic neglect of and violence toward black subjects, Beyoncé does not suggest black subjects cannot speak for themselves, but rather that they have spoken and have not been heard. Beyoncé does not offer a new language or claim a position of authority, but rather calls for unity in the continued, collective protest of the injustices she draws renewed attention to using her unique celebrity status. Secondly, to critique Beyoncé, presumably for speaking for others, also denies or questions her own agency to speak for herself. Beyoncé defies the lack of representation of black women in Western popular culture, while also speaking as a successful black woman within that culture. She infuses her images of female blackness with an honesty about her present status and lifestyle, while asserting lyrically that she is irrevocably of the culture whose lack of recognition she seeks to correct. She sings about her success as attainable and deserved, identifies herself with various slang terms for people of color, and maintains a relatability through unpretentious cultural references to hot sauce, Red Lobster, and Cuervo tequila, among other examples.

By creating nine distinct personas throughout the video, she represents several gendered, black cultural territories that lie between the common "country" Southern culture Beyoncé Knowles asserts she comes from, having grown up in Houston, Texas, and the high, privileged society in which she finds herself as half of the billion-dollar empire she shares with her rap-mogul husband Jay-Z. Each character serves a specific purpose while also expressing an overriding fluidity of identity through performance. Before we examine the symbolism of several of her figures, however, I would like to consider how the portrayal of these various roles fits within an ontological multiplicity explored in discourse on black subjectivity. Bringing these discourses into view further highlights the subversion of class and gender in Beyoncé's performative strategy.

While Beyoncé's performance in *Formation* elevates common Southern black culture by way of her celebrity, it is also worth noting the irony of preserving and performing these elements of her cultural identity, which, as part of her promotional economy, maintain her current, privileged status, and thus the divide between herself and the majority of her fan base. This could, in fact, be said of any successful promotional album cycle, however this is particularly pertinent given the level of success of *Lemonade*,[43] and how distant Beyoncé's upper-class reality must be from that of the disenfranchised communities documented in the *Formation* video. Beyoncé produces a splintered self which must acknowledge her high cultural reality in the video through designer dresses and custom cars, while exploiting her pre-fame self as a way of confirming authenticity and a connection to the cultures she presents in the video. Furthermore, we might consider how these representations of race and class are complicated by sex.

In her observation of black female authors, Mae Gwendolyn Henderson writes:

Black women writers enter into testimonial discourse with black men as blacks, with white women as women, and with black women as black women. At the same time, they enter into a competitive discourse with black men as women, with white women as blacks, and with white men as black women. Black women must speak in a plurality of voices as well as in a multiplicity of discourses.[44]

While Du Bois identified the role of the white Other in constructing black (male) subjectivity, Henderson notes this continual struggle among black female authors to identify themselves through a more complex navigation of dominant racial and sexual hierarchies. She calls this ability to change one's voice or discourse depending on who is being spoken to, "multi-vocality." Beyoncé employs Henderson's model through her proliferation of identities, speaking as and to various subjects. Moreover, the queer and feminist figures she introduces to this landscape further compound the points of identification to and from which subjects communicate. Whereas Beyoncé may at times be speaking as a woman, to women, or as a black woman, to black women, Big Freedia's multi-vocalities extend to trans women, queer women, queer men. In the character analyses below we will observe the identities Beyoncé performs, the nuance of their individual signification, and how, despite speaking in a myriad of tongues, *Formation* culminates in a message and performance of solidarity.

In her first role, Beyoncé wears a simple red housedress. Her hair is pulled back, but frizzes around her face. She wears no makeup. Her seemingly domestic femininity is subverted through the dress' pairing with masculine combat boots and her authoritative stance atop a New Orleans police cruiser, which slowly sinks into the flooded waters beneath her. Beyoncé stands, in Brechtian terms, "between the spectator and event."[45] She does not dramatize a role as a victim of Hurricane Katrina, but instead incorporates it as her backdrop to familiarize her audience with the themes pursued in the video.

Though seemingly plain, her ensemble also reveals her class: her dress and boots are designed by high-fashion labels Gucci and Louis Vuitton respectively. The languid comfort of her poses reads as dismissive to the "haters" she addresses and insults as "corny" in her first line of the song. She then tells the paparazzi to, "catch [her] fly and [her] cocky fresh."[46] Despite referencing the paparazzi in designer clothes while also lowering into the water, she remains unaffected and casual. With this image Beyoncé occupies high and low roles. She plays the casual but fashionable icon who could sink white authority under the weight of her feminine blackness.[47]

The reading of the next of Beyoncé's characters chimes with the work of Cathy Cohen, who identifies participating in codes of respectability and expected behaviours as a way of assimilating to the very culture which marginalizes people of color, and thus as compromising of the politics she promotes in her text "Deviance as Resistance." Cohen explains that the, "approach to queering African American Studies that [she] advocates is one based in an expansive understanding of who and what is queer and is, therefore, rooted in ideas such as deviance and agency and not exception and inclusion."[48] Cohen advises against a politics of inclusion. Rather, hers is a politics of celebrating and politicizing difference. Beyoncé exemplifies this through her handling of her relationships and sexuality, and her creation of a specifically black space throughout *Formation*. She also promotes alternative bonds outside of the nuclear family structure that she suggests people (specifically women) must activate, and lyrically combats a heteronormative relationship model, further reflective of deviant queer tones of the work.

Deviant elements of Beyoncé's performance are largely manifested in a character that is widow-like, dressed in all black, with her neck, chest, wrists and fingers completely covered in diamond jewelry. She stands in front of a Southern Gothic mansion flanked by men who appear to be the formally dressed staff of the home. When the character is shown throughout the video, she nods cryptically to the beat of the music. Her brimmed hat sits low on her face, covering her eyes. She looks both mysteriously domineering and mournful. Beyoncé asserts the character's deviant, anti-heteronormative identity despite her extravagant house and clothes, and the viewer's presumed knowledge of her marriage to and children with Jay-Z when she sings, "When he fuck me good I take his ass to Red Lobster."

There are two ways of reading this verse: either that she is speaking about her husband or about a lover. Nuanced meaning is created from each version, though both posit her as the authoritative figure in the relationship, thus subverting normative gender roles and heteronormative relationships. If the character she speaks about is a lover outside her marriage it subverts traditional monogamy. Despite this, she reinforces her role as wife and mother in other parts of the song,[49] essentially highlighting the sexual necessity for her deviance rather than a dissatisfaction with her husband or child. The privilege given to her sexual satisfaction opposes the classical expectation of demure femininity — especially in the South, where Beyoncé has laid her scene, and where historical archetypes such as "The Southern Belle" have dictated particularly rigid and limited gender identities.

Later passages in the song perpetually highlight her deviance as a dominant black female. Appropriating a kind of "Sugar Daddy" role, she also rewards her lover when he satisfies her sexually, with a mix of high and low gifts such as Red Lobster dinners and "Js" (Air Jordan Nike sneakers), and rides in her helicopter. The line, "I might get your song played on the radio station" suggests that she might use her power to build a man's career, or that she holds the power to her husband's continued success. She "might" get his song played on the radio. Her delivery suggests it depends on her level of satisfaction with her partner. She then suggests that "[he] just might be a black Bill Gates in the making." She re-considers, and reminds us of her position of power: "I just might be a black Bill Gates in the making."

At one point the character holds two red, manicured middle fingers up to the camera [Figure 29]. The subversive marriage of crassness with femininity expresses a total and unaffected lack of caring. The moment signifies just how indifferent the character is to any judgement that good fucking and cheap seafood are not sources of pleasure, ones commensurate with her status, or what is expected to satisfy a woman of her apparent class.

Figure 29: Beyoncé, *Formation*, 2016

Beyoncé lifts the brim of her hat for the last line of the song, finally making eye contact with the camera as she asserts, "You know you that Bitch when you cause all that conversation / Always stay gracious, best revenge is your paper."[50] Beyoncé acknowledges that provoking dialogue makes her powerful. Her gritty language subverts the formalities of the upper-class landscape where she wears diamonds and couture gowns, but stays gracious in spite of her self-made "paper" fortune. Meanwhile, her deviance is expressed through ambiguous sexual relationships marked by female authority.

In two additional scenes, Beyoncé costumes herself in more casual dress, but retains a glamorization consistent with her other characters. In one shot she appears hanging out of the passenger-side window of a "lowrider"-style El Camino car. Her hair is braided in cornrows. The car circles around an abandoned parking lot while Beyoncé leans out the window, drawing our focus to her hair and a sense of freedom expressed by her outstretched arms and closed eyes [Figure 30]. In the second of her street scenes, she is accompanied by several female backup dancers of color. They wear casual but sexy denim outfits, dancing in unison, physically enacting Beyoncé's choral refrain: "OK ladies, now let's get in formation." The call for togetherness doubles as a call to get "information." She invites others, specifically "Ladies," and implicitly black ladies, to organize and join her.

Figure 30: Beyoncé, *Formation*, 2016

Alongside her backup dancers, Beyoncé forms a non-violent "gang" of women who peacefully occupy street space, historically perceived as masculine and potentially violent. The image also subverts the historical alignment of women in the street with prostitution. In her essay "Settling Accounts with Subcultures: A Feminist Critique," Angela McRobbie identifies this tactic in Pat Benatar's 1983 *Love is a Battlefield* video, which pictures similar female dance sequences in urban street space. McRobbie reminds us that, "the street remains in some ways taboo for women (think of the unambiguous connotations of the term street walker)."[51] Significant to this discourse is the consideration that, disappointingly, since McRobbie's writing in 1983, the stigma she explores has remained fairly unchanged. "Formation" considers in its lyrics and dramatizes in the video the power of black women uniting as a system of support, a source of knowledge, and re-claiming stigmatized space, and desire.

The last of the video's identities I wish to address exposes how Beyoncé manipulates temporality to subversive effect. As with the visual and lyrical pairing mentioned earlier, where chain restaurants and chopper helicopters exist in the same reality as a woman seemingly depicted from the historic South, Beyoncé makes constant visual reference to *the* past and *her* past.

In stark contrast to the confrontational character in all black, Beyoncé also plays two Antebellum-style Southern belles in all white. One twirls a parasol in a high-collar white blouse and corset. The other is surrounded by a bevy of black women who fan themselves in long formal dresses [Figure 31]. She suggests a reconfigured history through the display of classical portraits of black women hung behind the group. She reinforces through her lyrics that her blackness and background maintain an authenticity reflective of black experience.

Over these scenes, she sings:

My daddy Alabama, my momma Louisiana
You mix that negro with that Creole, make a Texas Bama
I like my baby heir with baby hair and afros
I like my negro nose with Jackson Five nostrils
Earned all that money, but they never take the country out' me.
I got hot sauce in my bag. Swag.[52]

Figure 31: Beyoncé, *Formation*, 2016

This section takes an explicit ownership of black physicality. Beyoncé refers to herself as a "Bama" — a derogatory Southern slang term. At another point in the song she self-references as a "Yellow-bone," another slur for light-skinned black women. She expresses pride in natural, unaltered blackness: "Jackson Five" (rather than Michael Jackson) nostrils, and the natural afro hairstyle worn by her daughter in the video. It is this passage which makes this pop song operate differently than most because it demands that we question who it is for, and perhaps take the liberty of saying that it is not for some audiences.

In the days following the release of *Formation* this topic of ownership was explored across dozens of popular online platforms. Allison P. Davis wrote for *New York Magazine*:

I'm coming down firmly on the side that says this song is not for everyone.

Let me be clear: It is for everyone to download, listen to, think about, learn from, and discuss. But it is not for everyone to take ownership over: This song, and its message, <u>belongs to black people</u>. And everyone needs to be okay with the fact that some moments in pop culture mean more to one group of people than to others. "Formation," with its <u>rare message</u> of unabashed black female pride, is one of those moments.[53]

What I read from this declaration is that, as a black woman, the author feels that *Formation* is part hers — that a fear of misinterpretation or appropriation has inspired her protective tone. She not only takes ownership, but suggests that ownership be denied to non-Black audiences, who instead are meant to, "download, listen, think, learn from, and discuss" the song, but not sing along to or self-reflect in it. University of Waterloo professor Naila Keleta-Mae, who teaches an entire course dedicated to the subject of Beyoncé, explained in her article for music site *Noisey*:

Formation is a notably <u>complex meditation on female blackness</u>, the United States of America, and Capitalism. And the blackness that this song and video articulates is not some kind of abstract, cool, costume that can be put on and taken off at will. This female blackness is specific. It's 26 brown-skinned black women of multiple shades and shapes dancing in step. It's dark basements and large mirrors where queer black male hips twerk and revel. It's sun aversion, high collared dresses, corsets, and spread thighs. It's Messy Mya's voice from the grave asking what happened to New Orleans. It's black women's braless breasts bouncing in hallways lined with bookshelves and brocade. It's homes underwater because 11 years ago Hurricane Katrina broadcasted to the world that systemic and institutionalised anti-black racism was still state-sanctioned and real. *Formation* is

Big Freedia, the queen of bounce music, announcing on behalf of Beyoncé and herself that, "I did not come to play with you hoes / I came to slay, bitch." It's Gucci Spring '16, Chanel pre-fall, vintage, and custom clothing [...] In "Formation," black women's bodies are literally choreographed into lines and borders that permit them to physically be both inside and outside of a multitude of vantage points. And what that choreography reveals is the embodiment of a particular kind of 21st Century black feminist freedom in the United States of America; one that is ambitious, spiritual, decisive, sexual, Capitalist, loving, and communal.[54]

Keleta-Mae does not go as far as Davis' suggestion that the song is specifically not for all audiences, but pridefully catalogues the moments that are emblematic of black culture throughout the video. Also of note is how she authenticates Beyoncé's blackness by maintaining that these elements are not "costumes" one can take off. Rather, she suggests that the specificity of the images makes them intimate reflections of the black experience, each with long-standing histories, perhaps only legible to black audiences. Though Keleta-Mae's analysis reinforces many of my own assertions about *Formation*'s merits, I believe it is precisely the performance — the carefully chosen costumes Beyoncé dons in order to create personas, and how she employs those characters in fortified roles — that solidifies the power of these black, queer, and feminist representations. These tokens of blackness existed and were legible before Beyoncé incorporated them into the video, though perhaps it is precisely because she incorporates

them that they are validated, glamorized, and enough —
there is no need to pander to white culture that may not
identify with these images. I highlight this distinction, not
to undermine these tokens of blackness as lacking value in
their own right, but rather to return to the idea of finding
agency in performance. Just as gender can be performed in
endless ways, as we explored in the first chapter, *Formation*
exemplifies how blackness may be performed to queer and
feminist effect. Lastly, in her blog, "New South Negress,"
Dr Zandria Robinson offered the following analysis of the
video:

> Beyoncé places her own reckless, country blackness–
> one of afros, cornrows, and negro noses, brown liquor
> and brown girls, hot sauce, and of brown boys and
> cheddar bay biscuits–in conversation with, and as
> descended from, a broader southern blackness that is
> frequently obscured and unseen in national discourses,
> save for as (dying, lynched, grotesque, excessive)
> spectacle. *Formation*, then, is a metaphor — a black
> feminist, black queer, and black queer feminist theory
> of community organizing and resistance. To slay the
> violence of white supremacist heteropatriarchy, we
> must start, Beyoncé argues, with the proper formation.
> The proper formation is, she contends, made possible
> by the participation and leadership of a blackness on
> the margins.[55]

I assert that part of the inclination of black audiences
to identify with *Formation* is its absence of what Robinson
calls the "spectacle" of dying, lynched, grotesque black

bodies; in other words: victims. Beyoncé calls attention to the victimhood of New Orleans through her allusions to Hurricane Katrina, but the fortified and fearless bodies on view oppose the sentimental images typically scrolled across television news casts and national papers meant to elicit sympathy and grief. By including these texts I am hoping to draw attention to the revelatory and celebratory tones reflected through the relationship made to this work by female black audiences. Those tones, moreover, are manifested into the kind of provocative black female discourse necessary to combat the same homogenous white patriarchy that, as Robinson asserts, Beyoncé's radical art, and those that feel positively represented by it, could aid in dismantling.

In contrast to these exuberant reviews by black female fans who double as accredited scholars and authors, however, are severe criticisms from black feminist scholar bell hooks. In an entry on her blog titled "Moving Beyond Pain," hooks dismisses the idea of ownership through her leveling classification of the work as commodity: anyone may buy in. She fairly re-interprets aesthetics as marketing strategy and reminds us there's a bottom line. She draws parallels between Beyoncé's commodified body and slavery. Though she concedes that the subject matter is daring for its normalization and celebration of the black body at its center, she claims this, "does not truly overshadow or change conventional sexist constructions of black female identity."[56]

I find it difficult to reconcile some of her praise against her critique that the bodies used to populate this proposed world are mere commodities. Does she suggest that these women are for sale, or simply that their value is used to market the album? The lack of clarification reads fairly irresponsibly. Beyoncé is not for sale, nor are the women employed for their artistry and craft in *Formation* or throughout *Lemonade*. *Lemonade* is for sale, but hooks' argument that black female bodies are used to market the album is predicated on their perceived value, which significantly not all audiences might ascribe to such women, or these particularly fortified representations of them. hooks fails to interrogate the effect of *Lemonade* on such an audience.

Another facet to the discussion of the song's themes of black pride and ownership were assertions that "Formation" alienated white audiences. Though a colloquial example, this was explored by the American sketch comedy show *Saturday Night Live* in a clip that went viral online and arguably reflected the veritable phenomenon that the debate turned into. In the clip, chaos breaks out among white subjects who realize for the first time, after the release of *Formation*, that Beyoncé is black. The revelation is in fact portrayed as apocalyptic: traffic piles up as screaming drivers exit their vehicles to run, or pray in the street, while office workers hide under their desks following a power outage. In a state of frantic bewilderment, a white male character hesitantly suggests, "Maybe this song isn't for us." A white female co-worker replies in shock, "But usually everything is." Though the clip is meant as trivial TV satire, it addresses a systemic white privilege and entitlement that spans into realms as seemingly a-political as dance music. The fact that the subject could be satirized in such a way, let alone achieve viral circulation, stands to suggest that a significant number of people would get the joke. The identity politics brought to the fore are further complicated when a man asks, "How can she be black? She's a woman." To this a colleague responds in horror, "I think she might be both." The subtext here is that black women do not exist — they are not visible, they do not matter, they are not Beyoncé. If, as the sketch suggests, Beyoncé's blackness is a revelation to her white audience, *Formation* is not just of note for its feminist performance of blackness, but Beyoncé's refusal to play or present as white — something Beyoncé has been both accused of and conjectured to have been made a victim of by media who control her image.

The clip's suggestion that the track alienates a white audience through its explicit acknowledgement of blackness further suggests that music must therefore cater to white audiences. The examples we have explored above only further reinforce this idea that artists' blackness must not be spoken of, or physically too apparent, lest white audiences are no longer able to align themselves with the artists and their work. In his book *White: Essays on Race and Culture*, Richard Dyer explains that, "The invisibility of whiteness as a racial expression is of a piece with its ubiquity."[57] Dyer handles whiteness as the norm that is ironically invisible. He contends that as it remains invisible, it also remains the norm. *Formation* highlights Dyer's thesis. By making a video whose representations operate outside the norm, it highlights what exactly that norm is: the invisible whiteness that must not be mentioned, but is nevertheless catered to as standard. Through its prideful enunciations of black physicality, *Formation* brings that seldomly-felt discomfort and disorientation of a white audience's inability to self-identify to the fore. However, I argue that *Formation* is not meant to alienate in a true sense — to repel its white viewers — but rather to engage them intellectually with the social problems it potently dramatizes. This is perhaps best highlighted by reading *Formation* through Bertolt Brecht's fittingly titled "alienation theory" or "distancing effect."

As discussed earlier, Brecht's theater is one that caters to rationale. Unlike traditional theater or narrative film, Brecht's epic theater does not seek to immerse the audience in a fictional narrative in which they are meant to emotionally invest or self-identify. Indeed, like *Formation*'s allusions to Hurricane Katrina, Brecht often emphasizes the value of dramatizing historical events, creating more specific and objective narratives, rather than what he perceives as the falsity of "universal," "eternally human," themes, which purport to be natural in fictional scripts.[58] Brecht does not deny the emotion caused by the epic theater entirely, but considers the emotional response one might have to revelations of modern science as a comparable experience to the feelings produced by epic theater.[59] He privileges sign and symbol over character, and denounces the illusion of theatrical space. By often speaking to the audience in direct address, Brecht's actors break the theoretical "fourth wall," separating them from the audience.

Brecht's "distancing," or "alienation" effect promoted the development of an audience's consciousness through an independence from empathy. He maintained that such empathy is typically experienced at a passive level, when we easily identify with some element of the performance or character, particularly when centered around one of the aforementioned "universal themes" such as love, death, fortune, or misfortune — a strategy Brecht discredits in a theatrical context. Brecht asserts that "Theatrical forms correspond to particular trends of their time, and vanished with them. Similarly the modern epic theatre is linked with certain trends."[60] Though Brecht may not have envisioned his theory of distancing being applied to the analysis of pop music video, this quote expresses that he did have the foresight to anticipate changing modes of performance and how the epic theater might be adapted to it.

In *Formation*, Beyoncé announces her blackness, lyrically and visually, in literal and symbolic ways. Through an unexpected inability to identify with the pop star, the white audience must be forced to acknowledge blackness and examine the systems which continually reproduce white narratives. In this regard, Beyoncé strategically creates consciousness through the distancing of her white audience by invoking Brecht's alienation effect.

Unlike Beyoncé videos such as *Irreplacable* (2007) and *Halo* (2008), which present us with fictional narratives through which we are encouraged to empathize and identify with Beyoncé's heartbreak and romance, *Formation* does not solicit empathy. While her characters in *Irreplacable* and *Halo* express and elicit anger, longing, happiness, defeat, and arousal, for example, Beyoncé sings in direct address throughout *Formation*, maintaining an impenetrable façade of cool confidence. Rather than matching our emotions to those of Beyoncé's character narratives as we might have been encouraged to do in the aforementioned examples of past videos, with *Formation* we are forced to read the texts and signs she supplies to cull the meaning of her work. Those texts and signs hone in on specific black Southern cultures, communities and bodies; also occasionally even depicting specific periods of time.

The benefit of a failure of a white audience to identify with Beyoncé when, for example, she calls herself a "Texas 'Bama'" or a "Black Bill Gates-in-the-making" who "likes [her] negro nose with 'Jackson 5' nostrils," is to consider the infrequency of black representation in popular media — let alone representation of successful black women who also exert ownership of their sexuality — or simply the ubiquity of white representation that falsely, and silently, is meant to represent the experience of all.

X.

As a point of entry, *Formation* zooms in on the catastrophe of Hurricane Katrina, only to extend its endemic implications through a myriad of performed identities and temporalities. We are returned to the Antebellum South, where the delicacy of Beyoncé's Southern belles are subverted by the invisible histories of chattel slavery that rise into our consciousness. We are interrogated by voices of the dead, and implored by the living: "Stop shooting us." The violence alluded to in the video as having been produced by systemic racism, from slavery to Hurricane Katrina to the murder of Trayvon Martin, is combatted with expressions of gendered blackness that resist the silencing and fear symptomatic of racism, sexism, and homophobia: sweaty queer men twerk in NOLA dance halls, a line of afroed women flex their muscles in custom Gucci dance uniforms, while refrains alternate between calling for female unity and celebrating the physicality of blackness. Street authenticity and feminine glamor are traded equally in Beyoncé's representational economy, sanctioning the universal value of all black lives, regardless of status. In addition to exploring how these images' historical perspective suggest contemporary action, I have also considered how they evoke, challenge, or marry existing discourses in black studies. Perhaps most relevant to identifying the subversive power of performance in this video is Henderson's text on multi-vocality. Henderson highlights the precarity of various subjects within the singular black woman. This is shared in the work of Solange, Cakes da Killa, and Zebra Katz explored earlier in this section. Beyoncé relies on her performance to define how she speaks to and as these various subjects. Beyoncé's subversive project creates a series of tableaus fusing masculine, feminine, high, low, maternity, sexuality, unified strength and non-violent resistance. As evidenced by the various references to Black Lives Matter, it is of no coincidence that Beyoncé chose this critical moment in which to make a video whose expression of blackness is entirely unmatched in her catalog. Though the videos we explored earlier in the chapter — Solange's *Don't Touch My Hair*, Cakes da Killa's *Truth Tella*, and Zebra Katz's videos, *1 Bad Bitch* and *Blk Diamond* — do not make explicit reference to the movement, these works' queerness and feminism operates as inseparable from their blackness, affirming Black Lives Matter's mission toward greater visibility and acceptance of female, trans, and queer black lives.

X.

I flew from London to Paris for one day in order to finish this book at the hotel Royal Monceau, where Madonna filmed *Justify My Love*. The length of the trip was prescribed by the sudden limit placed on my time after being hired last-minute to start a teaching position in New York the following week. It was also cheaper than staying for any longer duration, especially since the value I had placed on my pilgrimage could be cashed in at the site; it wouldn't increase in parallel with the time spent there. I was hoping for feelings of proximity, which I did feel. I wanted to be where she was, perhaps touch, literally, even at some disgustingly microscopic level, that particular past. Though I must also admit that part of the desire to do this was to write about it — to make it a performance.

I was taken to rooms and walked the halls of the top floor where they shot the video. The rooms they filmed in have walls that cave in on the side because they are part of the roof. I kept seeing Madonna's unbalanced body swerving through the corridors, even though the hotel has since been completely redecorated. The walls are now covered with dizzying, thick, modern, black-and-white stripes, as is the carpet. Above the grand entry staircase are dozens of old-fashioned chandeliers, with tacky little lampshades and horrible chiffon bows on them. I felt a disorienting barrier of the present to the time and place I wanted to reach because, ironically, this present was marked by aesthetics that were dated, stuck somewhere grasping for a cutting edge of luxury domestic interiors that perhaps 2006 had regrettably prescribed.

I did not feel all of what I wanted to; all that I had planned to feel, because it didn't look like the video. I didn't feel like I was in the video, and were you there it would not have looked to you like I was in the video, which ultimately, was the image I wanted to put inside you with my words. The act only exists because I wanted you to see it, because in addition to the visual confusion of perhaps imagining me in that role, or at the very least having some of the allure of 1990s sex maven Madonna deflected onto me, I also liked the idea that an act of devotion could be a logical performance of completion (being in the place where something started, to finish the thing you have written about it). What makes it a performance rather than a story is that it was constructed, but also done. I will not lie about the performance to make it more beautiful, because this would undermine the act of having done it, which is fundamental to it being a performance, and is ironically what makes it real.

The objects of study explored in this book utilize performance to subvert gender and sex in music video. What this book proposes is that the power of performance to define and limit us can also be utilized to undo those restrictions and expose their construction. But, it has to be *done*. Importantly, when theorists such as bell hooks discredit the representational economy of an artist such as Beyoncé for her standing within a commercial landscape, they deny the subversive potential of performance to re-inscribe the body, its signification, and ultimately its experience and power.

The benefits of the internet to music video have been seen in the perpetually experimental representations of gender afforded by the medium's deregulation, and access to those images through the internet's veritable omnipresence. I return to a phrase of Richard Dyer, "cultural representations have real consequences for real people."[61] The online discourse produced in response to *Lemonade* highlights its power, and the power of work like it, to offer a re-telling of what our bodies signify.

In this book, subversive performances of gender were observed in dialogue with queer, feminist, and dramatic theories to locate subversive agency, and cull the meaning of these works. This research has been guided by the personal narrative that brought these schools of critical thought, and this particular medium into view. Since the launch of MTV in 1981 music videos have benefitted from technological advances, and have defied strident censorship. As we enter a new phase of conservatism, subversive work remains a necessity. Through performance, identity is weaponized against its own restrictions. At the site of music video this is achieved through visual extremity, and on a scale that is unmatched.

BIBLIOGRAPHY
X

Alfano, Sean. "Race An Issue in Katrina Response." *CBS News*. September 3, 2005. http://www.cbsnews.com/news/race-an-issue-in-katrina-response.

Anderson, Elijah. *Code of the Street: Decency, Violence, and the Moral Life of the Inner City*. New York: W.W. Norton and Co., 1999.

Andsager, Julie, and Kimberly Roe. "'What's Your Definition of Dirty, Baby?': Sex in Music Video." *Sexuality and Culture: An Interdisciplinary Quarterly*. Volume 7, Issue 3. (2003): 79-97.

Artaud, Antonin. *Oevres Complètes*. Paris: Èditions Gallimard, 1970.

Artaud, Antonin. *The Theater and Its Double*. New York: Grove Press, 1958.

Aufderheide, Pat. "Music Videos: The look of the Sound." *Journal of Communication*. Volume 36, Issue 1. (1986).

Auslander, Philip. *Liveness: Performance in a Mediatised Culture*. New York: Routledge, 1999.

Balaji, Murali. "'Vixen Resistin': Redefining Black Womanhood in Hip-Hop Music Videos." *Journal of Black Studies*. Volume 4, Issue 1. (2010): 5-20.

Barber, Stephen M., and David L. Clark. *Regarding Sedgwick: Essays on Queer Culture and Critical Theory*. New York: Routledge, 2002.

Barthes, Roland. *Camera Lucida: Reflections on Photography*. New York: Hill and Wang, 1981.

Bataille, Georges, and Allan Stoekl. *Visions of Excess: Selected Writings, 1927-1939*. Minneapolis: University of Minnesota Press, 1985.

Battan, Carrie. "We Invented Swag: NYC's Queer Rap." *Pitchfork*. March 21, 2012. http://pitchfork.com/features/article/8793-we-invented-swag/.

Baumgardner, Jennifer, and Amy Richards. *Manifesta: Young Women, Feminism, and the Future*. New York: Farrar, Straus and Giroux, 2000.

Baxter, Richard et Al. "A Content Analysis of Music Video." *Journal of Broadcasting and Electronic Media*. Volume 29, Issue 3. (1985): 333-340.

Bennett, Chad. "Flaming the Fans: Shame and the Aesthetics of Queer Fandom in Todd Haynes's Velvet Goldmine." *Cinema Journal*. Volume 49, Issue 2. (2010): 17-39.

Berger, Anne-Emmanuelle. *The Queer Turn in Feminism: Identities, Sexualities, and the Theater of Gender*. New York: Fordham University Press, 2014.

Berlant, Lauren. "Live Sex Acts (Parental Advisory: Explicit Material)." *Feminist Studies*. Volume 21, Issue 2. (1995): 379-404.

Bial, Henry. *The Performance Studies Reader*. London: Routledge, 2004.

Blau, Herbert. *Blooded Thought: Occasions of Theatre*. New York: Performing Arts Journal Publications, 1982.

Blau, Herbert. *Take Up the Bodies: Theater at the Vanishing Point*. Urbana: University of Illinois Press, 1982.

Blessing, Jennifer, and J. Jack Halberstam. *Rrose Is a Rrose Is a Rrose: Gender Performance in Photography*. New York: Guggenheim Museum, 1997.

Bollen, Jonathan. "Sexing the Dance at Sleaze Ball 1994." *Drama Review*. Volume 40, Issue 3. (1996): 166-191.

Bonnett, John. "Review: N. Katherine Hayles's How We Became Posthuman: Virtual Bodies in Cybernetics, Literature, and Informatics." *Journal of the Association for History and Computing*. Volume 3, Issue 3. (2000): 1-6.

Bost, Suzanne. "Be Deceived If Ya Wanna Be Foolish": (Re)constructing Body, Genre, and Gender in Feminist Rap." *Postmodern Culture*. Volume 12, Issue 1. (2001).

Brake, Michael. "Comparative Youth Culture: The Sociology of Youth Cultures and Youth Subcultures in America, Britain and Canada." *PsycCRITIQUES*. Volume 31, Issue 9. (1986).

Brandt, George W. *Modern Theories of Drama: A Selection of Writings on Drama and Theatre, 1850-1990*. Oxford: Clarendon Press, 1998.

Brannigan, Erin. *Dancefilm: Choreography and the Moving Image*. New York: Oxford University Press, 2011.

Brecht, Bertolt, and John Willett. *Brecht on Theatre; The Development of an Aesthetic*. New York: Hill and Wang, 1964.

Brill, Dunja. *Goth Culture: Gender, Sexuality and Style*. Oxford: Berg, 2008.

Burgess, Jean, Joshua Green, Henry Jenkins, and John Hartley. *YouTube: Online Video and Participatory Culture*. Cambridge, England: Polity, 2009.

Butler, Cornelia H., and Lisa Gabrielle Mark. *WACK!: Art and the Feminist Revolution*. Los Angeles: Museum of Contemporary Art, 2007.

Butler, Judith. *Bodies That Matter: On the Discursive Limits of "Sex."* New York: Routledge, 1993.

Butler, Judith. "Force of Fantasy: Feminism, Mapplethorpe, and Discursive Excess," *Differences: A Journal of Feminist Cultural Studies*. Volume 2, Issue 2. Durham: Duke University Press, 1990.

Butler, Judith. *Gender Trouble: Feminism and the Subversion of Identity*. New York: Routledge, 1990.

Butler, Judith. "Imitation and Gender Insubordination." *Inside/Out: Lesbian Theories, Gay Theories,* ed. Diana Fuss. New York: Routledge, 1991.

Butler, Judith, and Sara Salih. *The Judith Butler Reader*. Malden: Blackwell Pub, 2003.

Butler, Judith. "Performative Acts and Gender Constitution: An Essay in Phenomenology and Feminist Theory." *Theatre Journal*. Volume 40, Issue 4. (1988): 519-531.

Butler, Judith. *Undoing Gender*. New York: Routledge, 2004.

Björk.com. "The Light of Love." 2001. Accessed November 14, 2015. http://wayback.archive.org/web/20120930183924/http://unit.bjork.com/specials/gh/SUB-07/making/.

Caulfield, Keith. "Beyonce Scores Her Sixth Million-Selling Album in U.S. With 'Lemonade.'" *Billboard,* June 8, 2016. http://www.billboard.com/articles/columns/chart-beat/7400402/beyonce-lemonade-sixth-million-selling-album.

Centers for Disease Control and Prevention. "Epidemiologic Notes and Reports Acquired Immunodeficiency Syndrome (AIDS) among Blacks and Hispanics." Last modified May 2, 2001. http://www.cdc.gov/mmwr/preview/mmwrhtml/00000810.htm.

Chastagner, Claude. "The Parents' Music Resource Center: From Information to Censorship." *Popular Music.* Volume 18, Issue 2 (1999): 179-192.

Clarke, Deborah. *Driving Women: Fiction and Automobile Culture in Twentieth-century America.* Baltimore: Johns Hopkins University Press, 2007.

Cohen, Cathy. "Deviance as Resistance: A New Research Agenda for the Study of Black Politics." *Du Bois Review.* Volume 1, Issue 1. (2004): 27-45.

Collins, Patricia Hill. *Black Sexual Politics: African Americans, Gender, and the New Racism.* New York: Routledge, 2004.

Colothan, Scott. "Peaches Calls Gaga a 'Very Polished Diva.'" *Gigwise.* November 18, 2009. http://www.gigwise.com/news/53500/peaches-lady-gaga-is-a-very-polished-diva www.gigwise.com.

Dale, Catherine. "CRUEL: Antonin Artaud and Gilles Deleuze." *A Shock to Thought.* London: Routledge, 2002.

Davies, Bree. "Mykki Blanco." *West Word.* January 21, 2015. http://www.westword.com/music/mykki-blanco-you-will-have-your-breaking-points-but-you-must-persevere-6279290

Davis, Allison P. "Why Are White People Trying to Ruin 'Formation'?." *New York Magazine, The Cut.* February 26, 2016. http://nymag.com/thecut/2016/02/why-are-white-people-trying-to-ruin-formation.html.

Day, Aaron. "Lady Gaga: 'I've taken a few dips in the Lady Pond.'" *Pink News.* September 13, 2013. http://www. pinknews.co.uk/2013/09/12/lady-gaga-ive-taken-a-few-dips-in-the-lady-pond-lesbians-are-way-more-daring-than-straight-men/

DeBeauvoir, Simone. *The Second Sex.* New York: Knopf, 1953.

DeFrantz, Thomas, and Anita Gonzalez. *Black Performance Theory.* Durham: Duke University Press, 2014.

Diller, Edward. "Aesthetics and the Grotesque: Friedrich Dürrenmatt." *Wisconsin Studies in Contemporary Literature.* Volume 7, Issue 3. (1966): 328-35.

Dombal, Ryan. "Video: Perfume Genius 'Hood.'" *Pitchfork.* January 18, 2012. http://pitchfork.com/news/45133-video-perfume-genius-hood/.

Du Bois, W. E. B. *The Souls of Black Folks.* New York: Dodd, Mead, 1961.

Duggan, Lisa. *The Twilight of Equality?: Neoliberalism, Cultural Politics, and the Attack on Democracy.* Boston: Beacon, 2003.

Dürrenmatt, Freidrich. *Problems of the Theatre.* New York: Grove Press, 1964.

Dworkin, Andrea. "Against the Male Flood: Censorship, Pornography, and Equality." *Oxford Readings in Feminism: Feminism and Pornography.* ed. Drucilla Cornell. Oxford: Oxford University Press, 2000.

Dworkin, Andrea. *Pornography: Men Possessing Women.* New York: Perigee Books, 1981.

Dyer, Richard. *The Matter of Images: Essays on Representations.* London: Routledge, 1993.

Dyer, Richard. *White: Essays on Race and Culture.* New York: Routledge, 1997.

Dyhouse, Carol. *Glamour: History, Women, Feminism.* London: Zed Books, 2010.

Emerson, Rana A. "'Where My Girls at?': Negotiating Black Womanhood in Music Videos." *Gender & Society.* Volume 16, Issue 1. (2002): 115-135.

Escobedo Shepherd, Julianne. "Solange: A Seat at the Table." *Pitchfork.* October 5, 2016. http://pitchfork.com/reviews/albums/22482-a-seat-at-the-table/.

Evans, Elizabeth. *The Politics of Third Wave Feminisms: Neoliberalism, Intersectionality and the State in Britain and the US.* 2015.

Faludi, Susan. *Backlash: The Undeclared War against American Women.* New York: Crown, 1991.

Fitts, Mako. "'Drop It Like It's Hot': Culture Industry Laborers and Their Perspectives on Rap Music Video Production." *Meridians: Feminism, Race, Transnationalism.* Volume 8, Issue 1. (2008): 211-235.

Fitzmaurice, Larry. "Watch Perfume Genius' Dark, Powerful Video for 'Take Me Home.'" *Pitchfork.* October 5, 2012, http://pitchfork.com/news/48107-watch-perfume-genius-dark-powerful-video-for-take-me-home/.

France Respers, Lisa. "Why the Beyoncé Controversy is Bigger Than You Think." *CNN.* February 24, 2016. http://edition.cnn.com/2016/02/23/entertainment/beyonce-controversy-feat/.

Fredrickson, Barbara L., and Tomi-Ann Roberts. "Objectification Theory: Toward Understanding Women's Lived Experiences and Mental Health Risks." *Psychology of Women Quarterly.* Volume 21, Issue 2 (1997): 173-206.

Freidman, Betty. *The Feminine Mystique.* New York: W.W. Norton, 2001.

Friedman, Jaclyn, and Jessica Valenti. *Yes Means Yes: Visions of Female Sexual Power & a World Without Rape.* Berkeley, Calif: Seal Press, 2008.

Friend, David. "Q&A: Peaches on Queer Imagery and Getting Yanked from YouTube." *The Montreal Gazette.* September 13, 2016. http://montrealgazette.com/entertainment/qa-peaches-on-queer-imagery-and-getting-yanked-from-youtube.

Frisby, Cynthia M., and Jennifer Stevens Aubrey. "Race and Genre in the Use of Sexual Objectification in Female Artists' Music Videos." *Howard Journal of Communications.* Volume 23, Issue1. (2012): 66-87.

Frith, Simon, Andrew Goodwin, and Lawrence Grossberg. *Sound and Vision: The Music Video Reader.* London: Routledge, 1993.

Goodwin, Andrew. *Dancing in the Distraction Factory: Music Television and Popular Culture.* Minneapolis: University of Minnesota Press, 1992.

Gray, Richard J. *The Performance Identities of Lady Gaga: Critical Essays.* Jefferson, NC: McFarland, 2012.

Greer, Germaine. *The Female Eunuch.* London: Paladin Books, 1971.

Halberstam, Judith. *Female Masculinity.* Durham: Duke University Press, 1998.

Halberstam, Judith. *Gaga Feminism: Sex, Gender, and the End of Normal.* Boston: Beacon Press, 2012.

Halberstam, Judith. *In a Queer Time and Place: Transgender Bodies, Subcultural Lives.* New York: New York University Press, 2005.

Halberstam, Judith, and Ira Livingston. *Posthuman Bodies*. Bloomington: Indiana University Press, 1995.

Halberstam, Judith. *Skin Shows: Gothic Horror and the Technology of Monsters*. Durham: Duke University Press, 1995.

Halberstam, Judith. *The Queer Art of Failure*. Durham: Duke University Press, 2011.

Hall, Peter. "Bear With Me." *I.D. Magazine*. November, 1997. Bjork.com Archive. Accessed February 10, 2016. https://web.archive.org/web/20060821183307/http://unit.bjork.com/specials/gh/SUB -10/index.htm.

Hall, Stuart, and Doreen Massey. "Interpreting the Crisis." *Soundings: A Journal of Culture and Politics*, 44 (2010): 57-71.

Haraway, Donna. *Simians, Cyborgs, and Women: The Reinvention of Nature*. New York: Routledge, 1991.

Harvey, David. *A Brief History of Neo-Liberalism* Oxford: Oxford University Press, 2007.

Hawkins, Stan. *Queerness in Pop Music.* New York: Routledge, 2016.

Hayles, Katherine N. *How We Became Posthuman: Virtual Bodies in Cybernetics, Literature, and Informatics*. Chicago: Univeristy of Chicago Press, 1999.

Heins, Marjorie. *Sex, Sin, and Blasphemy: A Guide to America's Censorship Wars*. New York: New York, 1993.

Henderson, Mae G. *Speaking in Tongues and Dancing Diaspora: Black Women Writing and Performing*. New York: Oxford University Press, 2014.

Higginbotham, Evelyn Brooks. *Righteous Discontent: The Women's Movement in the Black Baptist Church, 1880-1920*. Cambridge, MA: Harvard University Press, 1993.

Hill Collins, Patricia. *From Black Power to Hip Hop: Racism, Nationalism, and Feminism*. Philadelphia: Temple University Press, 2006.

Hoby, Hermione. "Rappers and Rape: The Incredible Sound and Hateful Lyrics of Odd Future." *The Guardian*. May 8, 2011, https://www.theguardian.com/music/2011/may/08/odd-future-tyler-creator-rape.

Hoby, Hermione. "Zebra Katz: 'Creating a strong, black, queer male is something that needed to happen.'" *The Guardian*. May 25 2013. https://www.theguardian.com/music/2013/may/25/zebra-katz-interview-ima-read

hooks, bell. *Ain't I a Woman: Black Women and Feminism*. Brooklyn: South End Press,1981.

hooks, bell. *Black Looks: Race and Representation*. Boston: South End Press, 1992.

hooks, bell. *Feminist Theory from Margin to Center*. Boston: South End Press, 1984.

hooks, bell. "Moving Beyond Pain." *bell hooks institute*. May 9, 2016. http://www.bellhooksinstitute.com/blog/2016/5/9/moving-beyond-pain.

hooks, bell. *We Real Cool: Black Men and Masculinity*. New York: Routledge, 2004.

hooks, bell. *Yearning: Race, Gender, and Cultural Politics*. Boston: South End Press, 1990.

Hurley, Jennifer M. "Debate: Music Video and the Construction of Gendered Subjectivity (or How Being a Music Video Junkie Turned Me into a Feminist)." *Popular Music*. Volume 13, Issue 3. (1994): 327-338.

James, Robin. "Robo-Diva R&B": Aesthetics, Politics, and Black Female Robots in

Contemporary Popular Music." *Journal of Popular Music Studies*. Volume 20, Issue 4. (2008): 402-23.

Johnson, E. Patrick, and Mae Henderson. *Black Queer Studies: A Critical Anthology*. Durham: Duke University Press, 2005.

Jones, Amelia. *The Feminism and Visual Culture Reader*. London: Routledge, 2003.

Jonze, Tim. "In Bed With Beth Ditto." *The Guardian*. March 16, 2011. https://www.theguardian.com/global/2011/mar/16/in-bed-with-beth-ditto.

Josephs, Brian. "Q&A: Cakes da Killa Is a Part-Time Pink Moscato Connoisseur and a Full-Time Rapper." *Spin*. November 1, 2016. http://www.spin.com/2016/11/cakes-da-killa-hedonism-interview/.

Kaplan, E. Ann. *Rocking Around the Clock: Music Television, Postmodernism, and Consumer Culture*. New York: Routledge, 1988.

Kalof, Linda. "DILEMMAS OF FEMININITY: Gender and the Social Construction of Sexual Imagery." *The Sociological Quarterly*. Volume 34, Issue 4. (1993): 639-651.

Keleta-Mae, Naila. "Get What's Mine: 'Formation' Changes the Way We Listen to Beyonce Forever," *Noisey*, February 8, 2016. https://noisey.vice.com/en_uk/article/beyonce-formation-op-ed-super-bowl-performance-2016

Kroker, Arthur. *Body Drift: Butler, Hayles, Haraway*. Minneapolis: University of Minnesota Press, 2012.

Lawson, Richard. "Why Are There So Many Gay People on YouTube?." *Vanity Fair*. June26, 2015. http://www.vanityfair.com/culture/2015/06/youtube-digest-june-26.

Leibetseder, Doris. *Queer Tracks: Subversive Strategies in Rock and Pop Music*. Surrey, England: Ashgate, 2012.

Levande, Meredith. "Women, Pop Music, and Pornography." *Meridians: Feminism, Race, Transnationalism*. Volume 8, Issue 1. (2008): 293-321.

Lhooq, Michelle. *"Zebra Katz and Leila "Blk Diamond" Is a Hauntingly Beautiful Examination of Cruelty."* THUMP, July 17, 2015. https://thump.vice.com/en_uk/video/zebra-katz-and-leila-blk-diamond-is-a -hauntingly-beautiful-examination-of-cruelty

Lorde, Audre. *Sister Outsider: Essays and Speeches*. Berkeley, Calif: Crossing Press, 2007.

Lynskey, Dorian. "Mykki Blanco: 'I didn't Want to be a Rapper. I Wanted to be Yoko Ono.'" *The Guardian*. September 15, 2016. https://www.theguardian.com/music/2016/sep/15/mykki-blanco-i-didnt-want-to-be-a-rapper-i-wanted-to-be-yoko-ono.

Lyttle, John. "George Michael Arrested Over Lewd Act." *The Independent*. April 9, 1998. http://www.independent.co.uk/news/george-michael-arrested-over-lewd-act-1155246.html.

Marranca, Bonnie. "Performance World, Performance Culture." *PAJ: A Journal of Performance and Art*. Volume 10, Issue 3. (1987): 21-29.

Martin, Reid. E-mail message to author. April 14, 2016.

Marx, Karl. *Eighteenth Brumaire of Louis Bonaparte*. London: Pluto Press, 2002.

McClary, Susan. *Feminine Endings: Music, Gender, and Sexuality*. Minneapolis: University of Minnesota Press, 1991.

Mcgrath, John Edward. "Trusting in Rubber: Performing Boundaries during the AIDS Epidemic." *TDR: The Drama Review.* Volume 39, Issue 2. (1995): 21-38.

McRobbie, Angela. *Feminism and Youth Culture,"* Second Edition. London: Routledge, 1991.

Metro. "Lady Gaga: I'm not super sexy." January 21, 2009. http://metro.co.uk/2009/01/21/lady-gaga-im-not-super-sexy-357717/.

Mico, Stephen. "'I Want Muscles': House Music, Homosexuality and Masculine Signification." *Popular Music.* Volume 20, Issue 3. (2001). 359-378.

Milder, Patricia. "Staging the Image: Video in Contemporary Performance." *PAJ: A Journal of Performance and Art.* 31, no. 3 (2009): 108-119.

Millett, Kate. *Sexual Politics.* Garden City, N.Y.: Doubleday, 1970.

Moheno, Max. "Five Artists Tell Us About the Lasting Impact of 'Paris is Burning' 25 Years Later." *THUMP.* August 12, 2016. https://thump.vice.com/en_us/article/paris-is-burning-25-year-anniversary.

Montgomery, James. "Lady Gaga's 'Alejandro' Director Explains Video's Painful Meaning." *MTV,* June 9, 2010. http://www.mtv.com/news/1641136/lady-gagas-alejandro-director-explains-videos-painful-meaning/.

Moore, Madison. *How to be Beyoncé.* Williamsburg: Thought Catalog, 2013.

Mulvey, Laura. "Visual Pleasure and Narrative Cinema." *Screen.* Volume 16, Issue 3. (1975): 6-18.

Muñoz, José Esteban. Cr*uising Utopia: The Then and There of Queer Futurity.* New York: New York University Press, 2009.

Muñoz, José Esteban. *Disidentifications: Queers of Color and the Performance of Politics*. Minneapolis: University of Minnesota Press, 1999.

Muñoz, José. "The White to be Angry: Vaginal Davis's Terrorist Drag." *Social Text*. Issue 53, (1997): 80-103.

Murray, Nick. "Q&A: Le1f," *The Village Voice*, May 4, 2012. http://www.villagevoice.com/music/qanda-le1f-talks-the-influence-of-ballroom-and-working-with-das-racist-spank-rock-and-nguzunguzu-6603133.

Neilsen Sounscan. "Minority Viewership Drives Record Breaking Super Bowl XLIV." Febryary 12, 2010. http://www.nielsen.com/us/en/insights/news/2010/super-bowl-xliv-minority-viewership.html.

Neilsen Soundscan. "Super Bowl 50 Draws 111.9 Million TV Viewers, 16.9 Million Tweets." February 8, 2016. http://www.nielsen.com/us/en/insights/news/2016/super-bowl-50-draws-111-9-million-tv-viewers-and-16-9-million-tweets.html.

Nelson, Maggie. *The Art of Cruelty: A Reckoning*. New York: W.W. Norton & Co., 2011.

NME. "The Piercing Sound of Bjork." October 19, 2001 http://www.nme.com/news/music/bjork-188-1375717.

O'Dell, Kathy. *Contract with the Skin: Msochism, Performance Art, and the 1970s*. Minneapolis: University of Minnesota Press, 1998.

Owens, Craig. *Beyond Recognition: Representation, Power, and Culture*. Berkeley: University of California Press, 1992.

Parker, Heidi. "Mykki Blanco Talks Health Condition." *Daily Mail*. June 15, 2015. http://www.dailymail.co.uk/tvshowbiz/article-3124870/Mykki-Blanco-talks-health-condition-break-stigma-pride.html

Pearce, Sheldon. "Young Thug: Jeffery." *Pitchfork*. September 1, 2016 http://pitchfork.com/reviews/albums/22329-jeffery/.

Pat Pemberton. "10 Banned Music Videos." *Rolling Stone*. May 9, 2013. http://www.rollingstone.com/music/news/10-banned-music-videos-20130509.

Phelan, Peggy. *Acting Out: Feminist Performances*. Ann Arbor: University of Michigan Press, 1993.

Phillips, Layli; Kerri Reddick-Morgan and Dionne Patricia Stephens, "Oppositional Consciousness within an Oppositional Realm: The Case of Feminism and Womanism in Rap and Hip Hop, 1976-2004," *The Journal of African American History*. Volume 90, Issue 3. (2005): 253-277.

Railton, Diane, and Paul Watson. Music Video and the Politics of Representation. Edinburgh: Edinburgh University Press, 2011.

Roberts, Robin. *Ladies First: Women in Music Videos*. Jackson: University Press of Mississippi, 1996.

Rodger, Gillian. "Drag, Camp and Gender Subversion in the Music and Videos of Annie Lennox." *Popular Music*. Volume 23, Issue 1. (2004): 17-29.

Rohrer, Finlo. "Why Don't Black Americans Swim?." *BBC*. September 3, 2010.http://www.bbc.co.uk/news/world-us-canada-11172054.

Riviere, Joan. "Womanliness is a Masquerade." *Formations of Fantasy*. New York, NY: Routledge, 1986.

Roberts, Zandria. "We Slay, Part I." *New South Negress*. February 6, 2016. http://newsouthnegress.com/southernslayings/#more-733.

Russell-Cole, Kathy, et al. *The Color Complex: The Politics of Skin Color in a New Millennium*. Second edition. New York: Anchor Books, 2013.

Shafer, David. *Antonin Artaud*. London: Reaktion Books, 2016.

Schechner, Richard. *The Future of Ritual: Writings on Culture and Performance*. New York: Routledge, 1993.

Schechner, Richard and Lisa Wolford. *The Grotowski Sourcebook*. New York: Routledge, 1997).

Schechner, Richard. *Performance Theory*. London: Routledge, 2010.

Schippers, Mimi. "Recovering the Feminine Other: Masculinity, Femininity, and Gender Hegemony." *Theory and Society*. Volume 36, Issue 1. (2007): 85-102.

Schwichtenberg, Cathy. *The Madonna Connection: Representational Politics, Subcultural Identities, and Cultural Theory*. Boulder: Westview, 1993.

Sedgwick, Eve Kosofsky. *Between Men: English Literature and Male Homosocial Desire*. New York: Columbia University Press, 1985.

Sedgwick, Eve Kosofsky. *Epistemology of the Closet*. Berkeley, Calif: University of California Press, 2008.

Seidman, Steven. "Transfiguring Sexual Identity: AIDS & the Contemporary Construction of Homosexuality." *Social Text*. Volume 19, Issue 20. (1988): 187-205.

Sontag, Susan. "Approaching Artaud," in *Under the Sign of Saturn*. New York: Vintage Books, 1981.

Sontag, Susan. *A Susan Sontag Reader*. New York: Farrar, Straus, Giroux, 1982.

Straw, Will. "Music Video in Its Contexts: Popular Music and Post-Modernism in the 1980s." *Popular Music*. Volume 7, Issue 3. (1988): 247-66.

Taylor, Brandon. "Brooke Candy's Brand of Feminism." *Swide*. February 27, 2013. http://www.swide.com/art-culture/music-interview/brooke-candy-new-female-rapper-the-interview-in-milan/2013/2/27.

Taylor, Jodie. *Playing It Queer: Popular Music, Identity and Queer World-Making*. Bern: Peter Lang, 2012.

Telling, Gillian. "George Michael Says Coming Out Didn't Make His Life Easier." *People*. March 18, 2014. http://www.people.com/people/article/0%2C%2C20797971%2C00.html.

Vernallis, Carol. *Unruly Media: YouTube, Music Video, and the New Digital Cinema*. Oxford University Press, 2013.

Werde, Bill. "Lady Gaga 'Born This Way' Cover Story," *Billboard Magazine,* April 18, 2011.

Whaley, Natelegé. "Solange's 'Don't Touch My Hair' Is An Anthem Reclaiming Black Autonomy." *Huffington Post.* October 6, 2016. http://www.huffingtonpost.com/entry/solanges-dont-touch-my-hair-is-an-anthem-reclaiming_us_57f67383e4b030884674abca.

White, John J. *Bertolt Brecht's Dramatic Theory*. Rochester, N.Y.: Camden House, 2004.

Whiteley, Sheila, and Jennifer Rycenga. *Queering the Popular Pitch*. New York: Routledge, 2006.

Whiteley, Sheila. *Sexing the Groove: Popular Music and Gender*. London: Routledge, 1997.

Wilson, Benji. "Lady Gaga Gets Lippy," *The Daily Mail,* April 10, 2010. http://www.dailymail.co.uk/home/you/article-1264165/Lady-Gaga-gets-lippy-The-pop-star-teams-Mac-raise-Aids-awareness.html

Wolf, Naomi. *The Beauty Myth: How Images of Beauty Are Used against Women*. New York: W. Morrow, 1991.

Wright, Robert. "'I'd Sell You Suicide': Pop Music and Moral Panic in the Age of Marilyn Manson." *Popular Music*. Volume 19, Issue 3. (2000): 365-85

Zhang, Y., Miller, L.E., & Harrison, K. "The Relationship Between Exposure to Sexual Music Videos and Young Adults' Sexual Attitudes." *Journal of Broadcasting & Electronic Media*. Volume 52, Issue 3. (2008): 368-386.

DISCOGRAPHY

Beyoncé. "Formation." *Lemonade*. Parkwood Entertainment. Musical Recording. 2016.

Bjork. "Oceania." *Medulla*. Elektra Records. Musical Recording. 2004.

Khia. "My Neck, My Back." *Thug Misses*. Artemis Records. Musical Recording. 2002.

Nine Inch Nails. "Sin." *Pretty Hate Machine*. TVT Records. Musical Recording. 1989.

Ocean, Frank. "Bad Religion." *Channel Orange*. Def Jam Recordings. Musical Recording. 2012.

Ocean, Frank. "Thinkin' 'Bout You." *Channel Orange*. Def Jam Recordings. Musical Recording. 2012.

FILMOGRAPHY

Livingston, Jennie, Paul Gibson, and Jonathan Oppenheim. *Paris is Burning*. Burbank, CA: Miramax Home Entertainment, 1990.

VIDEOGRAPHY

Arca. *Anoche*. Directed by Jesse Kanda. Music Video, 3:47. 2017. https://www.youtube.com/watch?v=1YW94Psk0Jg.

Arca. *Reverie*. Directed by Jesse Kanda. Music Video, 3:17. 2017. https://www.youtube.com/watch?v=0WKWZ9y-dvU.

Arca. *Sad Bitch*. Directed by Jesse Kanda. Music Video, 2:09. 2015. https://imvdb.com/video/arca/sad-bitch.

Arca. *Sin Rumbo*. Directed by Jesse Kanda. Music Video, 3:35. 2015. https://www.youtube.com/watch?v=hE6OjTiMY3o.

Arca. *Thievery*. Directed by Jesse Kanda. Music Video, 2:44. 2014. https://imvdb.com/video/arca/thievery.

Banks, Azealia. *212*. Directed by Vincent Tsang. Music Video, 3:25. 2011. https://www.youtube.com/watch?v=i3Jv9fNPjgk.

Banks, Azealia. *Atlantis*. Directed by Fafi. Music Video, 2:08. 2012. https://imvdb.com/video/azealia-banks/atlantis.

Banks, Azealia. *Fierce*. Directed by Rony Alwin. Music Video, 3:17. 2013. https://www.youtube.com/watch?v=iMMzGrpL0K8.

Banks, Azealia. *Van Vogue*. Directed by Rankin. Music Video, 3:44. 2012. https://youtu.be/S2K1WkdaH2E.

Banks, Azealia. *Yung Rapunxel*. Directed by Jam Sutton. Music Video, 3:34. 2013. https://www.youtube.com/watch?v=iFe-sfJeh2E.

Beyoncé. 7/11. Directed by Beyoncé. Music Video, 3:37. 2014. https://imvdb.com/video/beyonce/711.

Beyoncé. *Formation*. Directed by Melina Matsoukas. Music Video, 4:53. 2016. https://imvdb.com/video/beyonce/formation.

Beyoncé. *Halo*. Directed by Philip Andelman. Music Video, 3:44. 2008. https://imvdb.com/video/beyonce/formation.

Beyoncé. *If I Were a Boy*. Directed by Jake Nava. Music Video, 5:04. 2008. https://imvdb.com/video/beyonce/if-i-were-a-boy.

Beyoncé. *Irreplaceable*. Directed by Anthony Mandler. Music Video, 4:12. 2007. https://imvdb.com/video/beyonce/irreplaceable.

Beyoncé. *Run The World (Girls)*. Directed by Francis Lawrence. Music Video, 4:51. 2011. https://imvdb.com/video/beyonce/run-the-world-girls.

Beyoncé. *Single Ladies (Put a Ring on It)*. Directed by Jake Nava. Music Video, 3:19. 2008. https://imvdb.com/video/beyonce/single-ladies-put-a-ring-on-it.

Beyoncé. *Video Phone*. Directed by Hype Williams. Music Video, 5:07. 2009. https://imvdb.com/video/beyonce/video-phone.

Björk. *Hunter*. Directed by Paul White. Music Video, 3:50. 1997. https://imvdb.com/video/bjork/hunter.

Björk. *Oceania*. Directed by Lynn Fox. Music Video, 3:39. 2004. https://imvdb.com/video/bjork/oceania.

Björk. *Pagan Poetry*. Directed by Nick Knight. Music Video, 4:03. 2001. https://imvdb.com/video/bjork/pagan-poetry.

Björk. *Unravel*. Directed by Lynn Fox. Music Video, 3:19. 2003. https://imvdb.com/video/bjork/unravel.

Björk. *Where is the Line*. Directed by Gabriela Frioriksdottir. Music Video, 4:41. 2005. https://imvdb.com/video/bjork/where-is-the-line.

Blanco, Mykki. *Coke White, Starlight*. Directed by Tristan Patterson. Music Video, 7:46. 2015. https://imvdb.com/video/mykki-blanco/coke-white-starlight.

Blanco, Mykki. *Initiation*. Directed by Ninian Doff. Music Video, 3:49. 2013. https://www.youtube.com/watch?v=w39Fxx10CEI.

Blanco, Mykki. *Loner*. Directed by Anthony & Alex. Music Video, 4:39. 2016. https://www.youtube.com/watch?v=IbPWe24jQ9A.

Blanco, Mykki. *She Gutta*. Directed by Jude Mc. Music Video, 5:53. 2014. https://www.youtube.com/watch?v=idpN3emg9e4.

Blanco, Mykki. *Wavvy*. Directed by Francesco Carrozzini. Music Video, 4:51. 2012. https://www.youtube.com/watch?v=sokeAMDm7mk.

Cakes da Killa. *Goodie Goodies*. Directed by Ja'Tovia Gary. Music Video, 3:14. 2013. https://imvdb.com/video/cakes-da-killa/goodie-goodies.

Cakes da Killa. *Talkin' Greezy*. Directed by Nico Bovat. Music Video, 3:16. 2016. https://www.youtube.com/watch?v=3orspcmY3cU.

Cakes da Killa. *Truth Tella*. Directed by Minister Akins. Music Video, 2:59. 2014. https://www.youtube.com/watch?v=X6OI-YJedao.

Candy, Brooke. *Das Me*.Directed by Brooke Candy and Matthew Boman. Music Video, 4:20. 2012. https://www.youtube.com/watch?v=dHULK1M-P08.

Candy, Brooke. *Living Out Loud*. Directed by Simon Cahn. Music Video, 4:19. 2017. https://www.youtube.com/watch?v=LFKRCIZ02J0.

Candy, Brooke. *Nasty*. Directed by Rankin. Music Video, 3:17. 2016. https://www.youtube.com/watch?v=GKr6A31pXH0.

Candy, Brooke. *Opulence*. Directed by Steven Klein. Music Video, 5:52. 2014. https://www.youtube.com/watch?v=CbChHPQhXtM.

Candy, Brooke. *Paper or Plastic*. Directed by Darren Craig. Music Video, 5:02. 2016. https://www.youtube.com/watch?v=g629WldXsf0.

Candy, Brooke. *Pussy Makes the Rules*. Directed by Meredith Danluck. Music Video, 3:52. 2013. https://www.youtube.com/watch?v=MDTViM1MXYw.

Candy, Brooke. *Rubber Band Stacks*. Directed by Cody Critcheloe. Music Video, 3:04. 2015. https://www.youtube.com/watch?v=Bg77h0ePeHQ.

Candy, Brooke. *Study in Duality*. Directed by Lil' Internet and Brooke Candy. Music Video, 2:44. https://www.youtube.com/watch?v=6PyLBc0bNDg.

Dr Dre. *Nothin' But a G Thang*. Directed by Andre Young. Music Video, 4:45. 1992. https://imvdb.com/video/dr.-dre/nothin-but-a-g-thang.

Fergie. *Big Girls Don't Cry*. Directed by Anthony Mandler. Music Video, 9:27. 2007. https://imvdb.com/video/fergie/big-girls-dont-cry-personal.

FKA twigs. *Glass and Patron*. Directed by FKA twigs. Music Video, 4:52. 2015. https://imvdb.com/video/fka-twigs/glass-patron.

Franz Ferdinand. *Michael*. Directed by Uwe Flade. Music Video, 3:25. 2004. https://imvdb.com/video/franz-ferdinand/michael.

Gossip. *Move in the Right Direction*. Directed by Price James. Music Video, 3:19. 2012. https://imvdb.com/video/gossip-1/move-in-the-right-direction.

Grimes. *Genesis*. Directed by Grimes. Music Video, 5:33. 2012. https://imvdb.com/video/grimes/genesis.

Grimes. *Oblivion*. Directed by Emily Kai Bock. Music Video, 4:11. 2012. https://imvdb.com/video/grimes/oblivion.

Haze, Angel. *Battle Cry*. Directed by Frank Borin. Music Video, 3:50. 2014. https://www.youtube.com/watch?v=QvvRNPOJPH0.

Haze, Angel. *Tribe Called Red*. Directed by Rollo Jackson. Music Video, 3:38. 2014. https://www.youtube.com/watch?v=HGEKm3NA9Is.

Haze, Angel. *Werkin' Girls*. Directed by BRTHR. Music Video, 3:10. 2012. https://www.youtube.com/watch?v=szj7efHG-00.

HIM. *Kiss of the Dawn*. Directed by Meiert Avis. Music Video, 3:56. 2007. https://imvdb.com/video/him/the-kiss-of-dawn.

Lady Gaga. *Alejandro*. Directed by Steven Klein. Music Video, 8:43. 2010. https://imvdb.com/video/lady-gaga/alejandro.

Lady Gaga. *Bad Romance*. Directed by Francis Lawrence. Music Video, 5:08. 2009. https://imvdb.com/video/lady-gaga/bad-romance.

Lady Gaga. *Beautiful and Dirty Rich*. Directed by Melina Matsoukas. Music Video, 2:48. 2008. https://imvdb.com/video/lady-gaga/beautiful-dirty-rich.

Lady Gaga. *Born This Way.* Directed byNick Knight. Music Video, 7:20. 2011. https://imvdb.com/video/lady-gaga/born-this-way.

Lady Gaga. *Just Dance.* Directed by Melina Matsoukas. Music Video, 4:07. 2008. https://imvdb.com/video/lady-gaga/just-dance.

Lady Gaga. *Lovegame.* Directed by Joseph Kahn. Music Video, 3:37. 2009. https://imvdb.com/video/lady-gaga/lovegame.

Lady Gaga. *Paparazzi.* Directed by Jonas Åkerlund. Music Video, 7:11. 2009. https://imvdb.com/video/lady-gaga/paparazzi.

Lady Gaga. *Perfect Illusion.* Directed by Andrea Gelardin and Ruth Hogben. Music Video, 3:05. 2016. https://imvdb.com/video/lady-gaga/perfect-illusion.

Lady Gaga. *Poker Face.* Directed by Ray Kay. Music Video, 3:35. 2008. https://imvdb.com/video/lady-gaga/poker-face.

Lady Gaga. *Telephone.* Directed by Jonas Åkerlund. Music Video, 9:31. 2010. https://imvdb.com/video/lady-gaga/telephone.

Lady Gaga. *Yoü and I.* Directed by Laurieann Gibson. Music Video, 6:22. 2011. https://imvdb.com/video/lady-gaga/youe-and-i.

Lambert, Adam. *For Your Entertainment.* Directed by Ray Kay. Music Video, 3:37. 2009. https://imvdb.com/video/adam-lambert/for-your-entertainment.

Lambert, Adam. *If I had You*. Directed by Brian Barber. Music Video, 3:57. 2010. https://imvdb.com/video/adam-lambert/if-i-had-you.

Le1f. *Boom*. Directed by Sam B. Jones. Music Video, 3:31. 2014. https://imvdb.com/video/le1f/boom.

Le1f. *Hush Bb*. Directed by Alex Da Corte. Music Video, 3:50. 2013. https://imvdb.com/video/le1f/hush-bb.

Le1f. *Koi*. Directed by Simon Ward. Music Video, 3:50. 2015. https://imvdb.com/video/le1f/koi.

Le1f. *Soda*. Directed by Sam B. Jones. Music Video, 2:57. 2013. https://www.youtube.com/watch?v=6herO1dIc4s.

Le1f. *Spa Day*. Directed by Jesse Miller-Gordon. Music Video, 4:24. 2013. https://imvdb.com/video/le1f/spa-day.

Le1f. *Sup*. Directed by Jesse Miller-Gordon. Music Video, 3:33. 2014. https://imvdb.com/video/le1f/sup.

Le1f. *Umami/Water*. Directed by Le1f. Music Video, 5:39. 2017. https://imvdb.com/video/le1f/umami-water.

Le1f. *Wut*. Directed by Sam B. Jones. Music Video, 2:49. 2012. https://imvdb.com/video/le1f/wut.

Lopez, Jennifer. *Ain't Your Mama*. Directed by Cameron Duddy. Music Video, 5:08. 2016. https://www.youtube.com/watch?v=Pgmx7z49OEk.

Lopez, Jennifer. *Booty*. Directed by Hype Williams. Music Video, 4:16. 2014. https://www.youtube.com/watch?v=nxtIRArhVD4.

Lopez, Jennifer. *I Luh Ya, Papi*. Directed by Jessy Terrero. Music Video, 5:17. 2014. https://www.youtube.com/watch?v=c4oiEhf9M04.

Lopez, Jennifer. *Same Girl*. Directed by Gomillion and Leupold. Music Video, 3:32. 2014. https://www.youtube.com/watch?v=s3T2A7xJgZs.

Lopez, Jennifer. *Waiting for Tonight*. Directed by Frances Lawrence. Music Video, 4:09. 1999. https://www.youtube.com/watch?v=_66jPJVS4JE.

Madonna. *4 Minutes*. Directed by Jonas & Francois. Music Video, 4:05. 2008. https://imvdb.com/video/madonna/4-minutes.

Madonna. *American Life*. Directed by Jonas Åkerlund. Music Video, 3:54. 2003. https://imvdb.com/video/madonna/american-life.

Madonna. *Bedtime Story*. Directed by Mark Romanek. Music Video, 4:27. 1995. https://imvdb.com/video/madonna/bedtime-story.

Madonna. *Bitch I'm Madonna*. Directed by Jonas Åkerlund. Music Video, 4:03. 2015. https://www.youtube.com/watch?v=7hPMmzKs62w.

Madonna. *Borderline*. Directed by Mary Lambert. Music Video, 3:59. 1984. https://imvdb.com/video/madonna/borderline.

Madonna. *Erotica*. Directed by Fabian Baron. Music Video, 5:14. 1992. https://imvdb.com/video/madonna/erotica.

Madonna. *Everybody*. Directed by Ed Steinberg. Music Video, 5:56. 1982. https://imvdb.com/video/madonna/everybody.

Madonna. *Express Yourself*. Directed by David Fincher. Music Video, 5:02. 1989. https://imvdb.com/video/madonna/express-yourself.

Madonna. *Frozen*. Directed by Chris Cunningham. Music Video, 5:23. 1998. https://imvdb.com/video/madonna/frozen.

Madonna. *Girl Gone Wild*. Directed by Mert Atlas and Marcus Piggott. Music Video, 3:50. 2012. https://www.youtube.com/watch?v=tYkwziTrv5o.

Madonna. *Give Me All Your Luvin'*. Directed by Megaforce. Music Video, 3:45. 2012. https://imvdb.com/video/madonna/give-me-all-your-luvin.

Madonna. *Hollywood*. Directed by Jean-Baptiste Mondino. Music Video, 3:58. 2003. https://www.youtube.com/watch?v=pGa3vDaydZQ.

Madonna. *Human Nature*. Directed by Jean-Baptiste Mondino. Music Video, 4:34. 1995. https://imvdb.com/video/madonna/human-nature.

Madonna. *Hung Up*. Directed by Johan Renck. Music Video, 5:27. 2005. https://imvdb.com/video/madonna/hung-up.

Madonna. *Justify My Love*. Directed by Jean-Baptiste Mondino. Music Video, 5:01. 1990. https://imvdb.com/video/madonsna/justify-my-love.

Madonna. *Like a Prayer*. Directed by Mary Lambert. Music Video, 5:38. 1989. https://imvdb.com/video/madonna/like-a-prayer.

Madonna. *Like a Virgin*. Directed by Mary Lambert. Music Video, 3:49. 1984. https://imvdb.com/video/madonna/like-a-virgin.

Madonna. *Material Girl*. Directed by Mary Lambert. Music Video, 2:21. 1985. https://imvdb.com/video/madonna/material-girl.

Madonna. *Music*. Directed by Jonas Åkerlund. Music Video, 4:47. 2000. https://imvdb.com/video/madonna/music.

Madonna. *Open Your Heart.* Directed by Jean-Baptiste Mondino. Music Video, 4:28. 1986. https://imvdb.com/video/madonna/open-your-heart

Madonna. *Papa Don't Preach.* Directed by James Foley. Music Video, 5:08. 1986. https://imvdb.com/video/madonna/papa-dont-preach.

Madonna. *Rain.* Directed by Mark Romanek. Music Video, 4:36. 1993. https://imvdb.com/video/madonna/rain.

Madonna. *Ray of Light.* Directed by Jonas Åkerlund. Music Video, 5:08. 1998. https://imvdb.com/video/madonna/ray-of-light.

Madonna. *Sorry.* Directed by Jamie King. Music Video, 4:22. 2006. https://www.youtube.com/watch?v=MyeN5h9nLas.

Madonna. *Vogue.* Directed by David Fincher. Music Video, 4:54. 1990. https://imvdb.com/video/madonna/vogue.

Manson, Marilyn. *Putting Holes in Happiness.* Directed by Philippe Grandrieux. Music Video, 4:00. 2007. https://imvdb.com/video/marilyn-manson/putting-holes-in-happiness.

Manson, Marilyn. *The Dope Show.* Directed by Paul Hunter. Music Video, 3:58. 1998. https://imvdb.com/video/marilyn-manson/the-dope-show.

M.I.A. *Bad Girls.* Directed by Romaine Gavras. Music Video, 4:11. 2012. https://imvdb.com/video/m.i.a./bad-girls.

Michael, George. *Faith.* Directed by Andy Morahan. Music Video, 3:44.1987. https://imvdb.com/video/george-michael/faith.

Michael, George. *I Want Your Sex.* Directed by Andy Morahan and George Michael. Music Video, 4:56. 1987. https://imvdb.com/video/george-michael/i-want-your-sex.

My Chemical Romance. *Helena*. Directed by Marc Webb. Music Video, 3:31. 2005. https://imvdb.com/video/my-chemical-romance/helena.

Nine Inch Nails. *Happiness in Slavery*. Directed by Jon Reiss. Music Video, 4:48. 1992. https://imvdb.com/video/nine-inch-nails/happiness-in-slavery.

Ocean, Frank. *Nikes*. Directed by Tyrone Lebon. Music Video, 4:56. 2016. https://imvdb.com/video/frank-ocean/nikes.

Ocean, Frank. *Thinkin' Bout You*. Directed by High6Collective. Music Video, 4:00. 2011. https://imvdb.com/video/frank-ocean/thinkin-bout-you.

Paramore. *Careful*. Directed by Brandon Chesbro. Music Video, 3:56. 2010. https://imvdb.com/video/paramore/careful.

Paramore. *Ignorance*. Directed by Honey. Music Video, 3:39. 2009. https://imvdb.com/video/paramore/ignorance.

Peaches. *Talk to Me*. Directed by Price James. Music Video, 3:26. 2009. https://imvdb.com/video/peaches/talk-to-me.

Perfume Genius. *Hood*. Directed by Winston H. Case. Music Video, 1:59. 2012. https://imvdb.com/video/perfume-genius/hood.

Perfume Genius. *Take Me Home*. Directed by Palo Duro. Music Video, 2:45. 2012. https://imvdb.com/video/perfume-genius/take-me-home.

Perry, Katy. *I Kissed a Girl*. Directed by Kinga Burza. Music Video, 3:05. 2008. https://imvdb.com/video/katy-perry/i-kissed-a-girl.

Pink. *Stupid Girls*. Directed by Dave Meyers. Music Video, 3:32. 2004. https://imvdb.com/video/pink/stupid-girls.

Salt-N-Pepa. *Let's Talk About AIDS*. Directed by Millicent Shelton. Music Video, 4:48. 1991. https://imvdb.com/video/salt-n-pepa/lets-talk-about-aids.

Salt-N-Pepa. *Let's Talk About Sex*. Directed by Millicent Shelton. Music Video, 4:48. 1991. https://imvdb.com/video/salt-n-pepa/lets-talk-about-sex.

Shakira. *Can't Remember to Forget You*. Directed by Joseph Kahn. Music Video, 3:25. 2014. https://www.youtube.com/watch?v=o3mP3mJDL2k.

Shakira. *She Wolf*. Directed by Jake Nava. Music Video, 3:48. 2009. https://www.youtube.com/watch?v=o3mP3mJDL2k.

Solange. *Cranes in the Sky*. Directed by Alan Ferguson and Solange. Music Video, 4:32. 2016. https://www.youtube.com/watch?v=S0qrinhNnOM.

Solange. *Don't Touch My Hair*. Directed by Alan Ferguson and Solange. Music Video, 4:24. https://www.youtube.com/watch?v=YTtrnDbOQAU.

SSION. *Earthquake*. Directed by Cody Critcheloe. Music Video, 5:12. 2012. https://imvdb.com/video/ssion/earthquake.

Star, Jeffree. *Beauty Killer*. Directed by Austin Young. Music Video. 2010. https://imvdb.com/video/jeffree-star/beauty-killer.

Star, Jeffree. Prom Night. Directed by Robby Starbuck. Music Video, 3:52. 2012. https://imvdb.com/video/jeffree-star/prom-night.

The Strokes. *The End Has No End*. Directed by Sophie Muller. Music Video, 2:59. 2004. https://imvdb.com/video/the-strokes/the-end-has-no-end.

TLC. *Ain't 2 Proud 2 Beg*. Directed by Lionel C. Martin. Music Video, 4:18. 1992. https://imvdb.com/video/tlc/aint-2-proud-2-beg.

West, Kanye. *Bound 2*. Directed by Nick Knight. Music Video, 4:14. 2013. https://imvdb.com/video/kanye-west/bound-2.

West, Kanye. *Fade*. Directed by Eli Linnetz. Music Video, 3:44. 2016. https://www.youtube.com/watch?v=IxGvm6btP1A.

West, Kanye. *Famous*. Directed by Kanye West. Music Video, 3:20. 2016. https://imvdb.com/video/kanye-west/famous.

West, Kanye. *Wolves*. Directed by Steven Klein. Music Video, 7:00. 2016. https://imvdb.com/video/kanye-west/wolves.

Young Thug. *Turn Up*. Directed by Garfield Larmond. Music Video, 3:34. 2016. https://www.youtube.com/watch?v=KJagA5R2wR8.

Zebra Katz. *1 Bad B*tch*. Directed by Nicklaus Lange. Music Video, 3:35. 2014.https://www.youtube.com/watch?v=XPbpl35uX8w.

Zebra Katz. *Blk Diamond*. Directed by Elvar Gunnarsson. Music Video, 3:00. 2015. https://imvdb.com/video/zebra-katz/blk-diamond

Zebra Katz. *Ima Read*. Directed by RUBEN XYZ. Music Video, 4:06. 2012. https://vimeo.com/34982652.

NOTES

PART ONE

1   Antonin Artaud, *The Theatre and Its Double*, trans. Mary Caroline Richards (New York: Grove Press, 1958), 85.

2   Ibid., 33.

3   Ibid., 36.

4   David A. Shafer, *Antonin Artaud* (London: Reaktion Books, 2016), 65.

5   Sontag, "Approaching Artaud," 27.

6   Antonin Artaud, *Oevres Complètes* (Paris: Gallimard, 1976), 124-5.

7   Roland Barthes, *Camera Lucida* (New York: Hill and Wang, 1981), 38.

8   Georges Bataille, *Visions of Excess: Selected Writings 1927-1939* (Minneapolis: University of Minnesota Press, 1985), 33.

9   Henderson, "Justify Our Love: Madonna and the Politics of Queer Sex," 123.

10 https://www.rollingstone.com/music/music-lists/express-yourself-the-making-of-madonnas-20-greatest-music-videos-140803/justify-my-love-1990-65232/

11 Ibid., 113.

12 Ibid., 111.

13 Ibid., 112.

14 Brecht, *Brecht on Theatre*, 122.

15 Walter Benjamin, *Understanding Brecht*, trans. Anna Bostock (London: Verso Books, 1998), 4-5.

16 Ibid., 71.

17 Judith Butler, "Imitation and Gender Insubordination," in *Inside/Out: Lesbian Theories, Gay Theories*, ed. Diana Fuss (New York: Routledge, 1991), 21.

18 Judith Butler, *Bodies That Matter: On the Discursive Limits of Sex* (New York: Routledge, 1993), 6.

19 Butler, *Gender Trouble*, 17.

20 Ibid., 15.

21 Butler, "Imitation and Gender Insubordination," 29.

22 Ibid.

23 Jennifer Blessing, "Gender Performance in Photography," in *Rrose is a Rrose is a Rrose: Gender Performance in Photography* (New York: Guggenheim Museum Publications, 1997), 15.

24 Jodie Taylor, *Playing it Queer: Popular Music, Identity, and Queer World Making* (Bern: Peter Lang, 2012), 14.

25 Ibid.

26 José Munoz, *Cruising Utopia: The Then and There of Queer Futurity* (New York: New York University Press, 2009), 1.

27 Ibid.

28 Andrea Dworkin, *Right-Wing Women* (New York: G.P. Putnam's Son, 1983), 77.

29 Paul B. Preciado, *Testo Junkie: Sex, Drugs, and Biopolitics*, trans. Bruce Benderson (New York: The Feminist Press at City University of New York, 2013), 338-339.

30 Donna Haraway, *Simians, Cyborgs, and Women: The Re-Invention of Nature* (New York: Routledge, 1991), 291.

31 Ibid., 292.

32   Ibid., 298.

33   Mae Gwendolyn Henderson, *Black Queer Studies: A Critical Anthology* (Durham: Duke University Press, 2005), 5.

34   James Montgomery, "Lady Gaga's 'Alejandro' Director Explains Video's Painful Meaning," *MTV*, June 9, 2010, http://www.mtv.com/news/1641136/lady-gagas-alejandro-director-explains-videos-painful-meaning/

35   Benji Wilson, "Lady Gaga Gets Lippy," *The Daily Mail*, April 10, 2010, http://www.dailymail.co.uk/home/you/article-1264165/Lady-Gaga-gets-lippy-The-pop-star-teams-Mac-raise-Aids-awareness.html

36   Deborah Clarke, *Women Driving: Fiction and Automobile Culture in Twentieth Century America* (Baltimore: John Hopkins University Press, 2007), 3.

37   Antonin Artaud, "The Theatre of Cruelty: The Second Manifesto," in *The Theory of the Modern Stage*, Ed. Eric Bentley (London: Pelican Books, 1968), 66.

38   Brandon Taylor, "Brooke Candy's Brand of Feminism," *Swide*, February 27, 2013, http://www.swide.com/art-culture/music-interview/brooke-candy-new-female-rapper-the-interview-in-milan/2013/2/27

39   Greer, *Female Eunuch*, 77.

40   Maggie Nelson, *The Art of Cruelty: A Reckoning* (New York: W.W. Norton & Co., 2011), 9.

41   Kathy O'Dell, *Contract with the Skin: Masochism, Performance Art, and the 1970s* (Minneapolis: University of Minnesota Press, 1998), 55.

42   Friedrich Dürrenmatt, *Problems of the Theatre* (New York: Grove Press, 1964), 47-48.

PART TWO

1   Though audiences are not able to upload their own content to Vevo, I have qualified the site as similar to YouTube for the ability offered to audiences to curate their own selection of content for viewing.

2   Vernallis, *Unruly Media*, 14.

3   Ibid.

4   Judith Butler, "Imitation and Gender Insubordination," in *Inside/Out: Lesbian Theories, Gay Theories,* ed. Diana Fuss (New York: Routledge, 1991), 13.

5   Ibid., 14.

6   Aaron Day, "Lady Gaga: 'I've taken a few dips in the Lady Pond,'" *Pink News*, September 13, 2013, http://www.pinknews.co.uk/2013/09/12/lady-gaga-ive-taken-a-few-dips-in-the-lady-pond-lesbians-are-way-more-daring-than-straight-men/

7   Butler, "Performative Acts and Gender Constitution," 520.

8   Artaud. *The Theater and Its Double*. 85.

9   Catherine Dale, "CRUEL: Antonin Artaud and Gilles Deleuze" in Brian Massumi, *A Shock to Thought* (London: Routledge, 2002) 5.

10 Bill Werde, "Lady Gaga 'Born This Way' Cover Story," *Billboard Magazine*, April 18, 2011, 4.

11 J. Jack Halberstam, *Gaga Feminism: Sex, Gender, and the End of Normal,* (Boston: Beacon Press, 2012), ix.

12 Ibid., 25.

13 Ibid.

14 Ibid., xii.

15 Germaine Greer, *The Female Eunuch* (London: Paladin Books, 1971), 38.

16 Ibid.

17 Jack Halberstam, *Female Masculinity* (Durham: Duke University Press, 1998), 6.

18 Ibid., 15.

19 Ibid., 5.

20 Butler, *Gender Trouble*, 174.

21 Andrea Dworkin, "Against the Male Flood: Censorship, Pornography, and Equality," in *Oxford Readings in Feminism: Feminism and Pornography*, ed. Drucilla Cornell, (Oxford: Oxford University Press, 2000) 30.

22 Marsha Meskimmon, "Conceptual Cartographies," in *WACK!: Art and the Feminist Revolution* (Cambridge, MA: MIT Press, 2001) 332.

23 Ibid.

24 Ryan Dombal, "Video: Perfume Genius *Hood,*" *Pitchfork,* January 18, 2012, http://pitchfork.com/news/45133-video-perfume-genius-hood/

25 Ibid.

26 Larry Fitzmaurice, "Watch Perfume Genius' Dark, Powerful Video for 'Take Me Home,'" *Pitchfork,* October 5, 2012, http://pitchfork.com/news/48107-watch-perfume-genius-dark-powerful-video-for-take-me-home/.

27 Frank Ocean. "Thinkin' 'Bout You," *Channel Orange,* Def Jam Recordings, Musical Recording, 2012.

28 Frank Ocean. "Bad Religion," *Channel Orange,* Def Jam Recordings, Musical Recording, 2012.

29 Hermione Hoby, "Rappers and Rape: The Incredible Sound and Hateful Lyrics of Odd Future," *The Guardian,* May 8, 2011, https://www.theguardian.com/music/2011/may/08/odd-future-tyler-creator-rape

30 Dorian Lynskey, "Mykki Blanco: 'I didn't Want to be a Rapper. I Wanted to be Yoko Ono,'" *The Guardian,* September 15, 2016, https://www.theguardian.com/music/2016/sep/15/mykki-blanco-i-didnt-want-to-be-a-rapper-i-wanted-to-be-yoko-ono

31 Sheldon Pearce, "Young Thug: Jeffery," *Pitchfork,* September 1, 2016, http://pitchfork.com/reviews/albums/22329-jeffery/

32 Carrie Battan, "We Invented Swag: NYC's Queer Rap," *Pitchfork,* March 21, 2012, http://pitchfork.com/features/article/8793-we-invented-swag/

33 Ibid.

34 Ibid.

35 Ibid.

36 Stan Hawkins, *Queerness in Pop Music,* (New York: Routledge, 2016), 274-275.

37 Ibid

38 Ibid

39 I would like to note that these figures have not been dealt with in this text due to the comparable lack of subversive gender representations in their video work.

40 Hawkins, *Queerness in Pop Music,* 266.

41 Bree Davies, "Mykki Blanco," *West Word,* January 21, 2015, http://www.westword.com/music/mykki-blanco-you-will-have-your-breaking-points-but-you-must-persevere-6279290

42 Heidi Parker, "Mykki Blanco Talks Health Condition," *Daily Mail*, June 15, 2015, http://www.dailymail.co.uk/tvshowbiz/article-3124870/Mykki-Blanco-talks-health-condition-break-stigma-pride.html

43 Hawkins, *Queerness in Pop Music*, 266

44 Dorian Lynskey, *The Guardian*

45 Jose Munoz, "The White to be Angry: Vaginal Davis's Terrorist Drag," *Social Text* 53 (1997): 91

46 Railton and Watson, *Music Video and the Politics of Representation*, 22.

47 N. Katherine Hayles, *How We Became Posthuman* (Chicago: University of Chicago Press, 1999), 3

48 Donna Haraway, *Simians, Cyborgs, and Women* (New York: Routledge, 1991), 316.

49 Carol Dyhouse, *Glamour: History, Women, Feminism* (London: Zed Books, 2010) 3.

50 Paula Rabinowitz, "Soft Fictions and Intimate Documents: Can Feminism be Posthuman" *Posthuman Bodies*, edited by Jack halberstam and Ira Livingston (Indianapolis: University of Indiana Press, 1995), 98.

51 http://www.dazeddigital.com/music/article/35172/1/watch-arca-reverie-video

52 Roberts, *Ladies First*, xxv.

53 Hayles, *How We Became Posthuman*, 3.

54 Jack Halberstam et al, *Posthuman Bodies* (Indianapolis: University of Indiana Press, 1995), 9.

55 Artaud, *The Theatre and its Double*, 10.

56 Halberstam et al, *Posthuman Bodies*, 19.

57 Judith Butler, "Force of Fantasy: Feminism, Mapplethorpe, and Discursive Excess," *Differences: A Journal of Feminist Cultural Studies*, Volume 2, Issue 2. (Durham: Duke University Press, 1990), 185.

58 Rabinowitz, "Soft Fictions," 97.

59 Dunja Brill, *Goth Culture: Gender, Sexuality, and Style Dress, Body, Culture* (Oxford: Berg Press, 2008)

60 Betty Freidman, *The Feminine Mystique,* (New York: W.W. Norton, 2001), 372.

61 Greer, *Female Eunuch,* 293.

62 "Hot 100 Songs — Year End Charts," *Billboard,* accessed June 1, 2014, http://www.billboard.com/charts/year-end/2007/hot-100-songs

63 Fergie, "Big Girls Don't Cry," *The Dutchess,* Interscope Records, 2006.

64 Michael Brake, *Comparative Youth Culture: The Sociology of Youth Cultures and Youth Subcultures in America* (London: Routledge & Kegan Paul, 1985), 166.

65 Katy Perry. "I Kissed a Girl," *One of the Boys,* Capitol Recordings, Musical Recording, 2008.

66 Lisa Dugan, *The Twilight of Equality? Neoliberalism, Cultural Politics, and the attack on Democracy,* (Boston: Beacon Press, 2003), 50.

67 Scott Colothan, "Peaches Calls Gaga a 'Very Polished Diva,'" *Gigwise,* November 18, 2009, http://www.gigwise.com/news/53500/peaches-lady-gaga-is-a-very-polished-diva www.gigwise.com.

68 Tim Jonze, "In Bed With Beth Ditto," *The Guardian,* March 16, 2011, https://www.theguardian.com/global/2011/mar/16/in-bed-with-beth-ditto.

69 David Harvey, *A Brief History of Neo-Liberalism* (Oxford: Oxford University Press, 2007), 19.

PART THREE

1   Researchers referred to the condition as "Gay-Related Immune Deficiency" after initial health reports were released in 1981. The use of the term, "AIDS" (Auto-Immune Deficiency Syndrome) was adopted in September, 1982.

2   "A Timeline of HIV/AIDS," Aids.gov. ,https://www.aids.gov/hiv-aids-basics/hiv-aids-101/aids-timeline/, (accessed April 7, 2017).

3   Jonathan Engel, *The Epidemic: A History of AIDS* (London: Harper Collins Publishers, 2006), 45.

4   Ibid.

5   Ibid.

6   Marjorie Heins, *Sex, Sin, and Blasphemy, a Guide to America's Censorship Wars* (New York: New Press, 1993), 188.

7   Claude Chastagner, "The Parents' Music Resource Center: From Information to Censorship," *Popular Music*, Volume 18, Issue 2. (1999): 190.

8   Lisa Henderson, "Justify Our Love: Madonna and the Politics of Queer Sex," in *The Madonna Connection: Representational Politics, Subcultural Identities, and Cultural Theory* (Boulder: Westview, 1993), 108.

9   Gillian Telling, "George Michael Says Coming Out Didn't Make His Life Easier," *People*, March 18, 2014, http://www.people.com/people/article/0,,20797971,00.html.

10 Butler, "Imitation and Gender Insubordination," 21.

11 "Epidemiologic Notes and Reports Acquired Immunodeficiency Syndrome (AIDS) among Blacks and Hispanics -- United States," *Center for Disease Control*, October 24, 1986, http://www.cdc.gov/mmwr/preview/mmwrhtml/00000810.htm, (accessed November 15, 2014).

12 Engel, *The Epidemic: A History of AIDS*, 76.

13 Suzanne Bost, "'Be Deceived If Ya Wanna Be Foolish': (Re)constructing Body, Genre, and Gender in Feminist Rap," *Postmodern Culture*, Volume 12, Issue 1. (2001): 38.

14 Leibetseder, *Queer Tracks*, 194.

15 It remains unclear whether Brown did, or did not raise his hands to surrender. Several witnesses claiming that he did raise his hands were ultimately discredited in the trial.

16 "About Black Lives Matter," *Black Lives Matter*, http://blacklivesmatter.com/about/, (accessed April 10, 2016).

17 Natelegé Whaley, "Solange's 'Don't Touch My Hair' Is An Anthem Reclaiming Black Autonomy," *Huffington Post*, October 6, 2016, http://www.huffingtonpost.com/entry/solanges-dont-touch-my-hair-is-an-anthem-reclaiming_us_57f67383e4b030884674abca

18 bell hooks, *Ain't I a Woman: Black Women and Feminism*, (Brooklyn: South End Press, 1981), 7.

19 Julianne Escobedo Shepherd, "Solange: A Seat at the Table," *Pitchfork*, October 5, 2016, http://pitchfork.com/reviews/albums/22482-a-seat-at-the-table/

20 Ibid.

21 Hawkins, *Queerness in pop music*, 46.

22 Max Moheno, "Five Artists Tell Us About the Lasting Impact of 'Paris is Burning' 25 Years Later," *THUMP*, August 12, 2016, https://thump.vice.com/en_us/article/paris-is-burning-25-year-anniversary.

23 Hawkins, *Queerness in pop music,* 46.

24 Dorian Corey, *Paris is Burning*, Directed by Jennie Livingston, (1990; New York, NY: Miramax, 2005) DVD.

25 bell hooks, *Black Looks: Race and Representation* (Brooklyn: South End Press, 1992), 147.

26 Hawkins, *Queerness in pop music,* 46.

27 Nick Murray, "Q&A: Le1f," *The Village Voice*, May 4, 2012, http://www.villagevoice.com/music/qanda-le1f-talks-the-influence-of-ballroom-and-working-with-das-racist-spank-rock-and-nguzunguzu-6603133.

28 Ibid.

29 Pepper LaBeija, *Paris is Burning*, Directed by Jennie Livingston, (1990; New York, NY: Miramax, 2005) DVD.

30 Brian Josephs, "Q&A: Cakes da Killa Is a Part-Time Pink Moscato Connoisseur and a Full-Time Rapper," *Spin*, November 1, 2016, http://www.spin.com/2016/11/cakes-da-killa-hedonism-interview/.

31 Hermione Hoby, "Zebra Katz: 'Creating a strong, black, queer male is something that needed to happen,'" *The Guardian*, May 25, 2013, https://www.theguardian.com/music/2013/may/25/zebra-katz-interview-ima-read

32 Michelle Lhooq, *"Zebra Katz and Leila's Blk Diamond Is a Hauntingly Beautiful Examination of Cruelty,"* THUMP, July 17, 2015, https://thump.vice.com/en_uk/video/zebra-katz-and-leila-blk-diamond-is-a-hauntingly-beautiful-examination-of-cruelty.

33 Ibid.

34 W.E.B. Du Bois, *The Souls of Black Folks* (Chicago: A.C. McClurg and Co., 1903), 2.

35 "Super Bowl 50 Draws 111.9 Million TV Viewers, 16.9 Million Tweets," *Neilsen Soundscan*, February 8, 2016, http://www.nielsen.com/us/en/insights/news/2016/super-bowl-50-draws-111-9-million-tv-viewers-and-16-9-million-tweets.html.

36 "Minority Viewership Drives Record Breaking Super Bowl XLIV," *Neilsen Sounscan*, Febryary 12, 2010, http://www.nielsen.com/us/en/insights/news/2010/super-bowl-xliv-minority-viewership.html.

37 Beyoncé, "Formation," *Lemonade*, Parkwood Entertainment, Musical Recording, 2016.

38 Ibid.

39 Sean Alfano, "Race An Issue in Katrina Response," *CBS News*, September 3, 2005, http://www.cbsnews.com/news/race-an-issue-in-katrina-response/

40 Ibid.

41 Dr. Zandria Roberts, "We Slay, Part I," *New South Negress*, February 7, 2016, http://newsouthnegress.com/southernslayings/#more-733

42 Reid Martin, e-mail message to author, April 14, 2016.

43 Keith Caulfield, "Beyoncé Scores Her Sixth Million-Selling Album in U.S. With *Lemonade*," *Billboard*, June 8, 2016, http://www.billboard.com/articles/columns/chart-beat/7400402/beyonce-lemonade-sixth-million-selling-album.

44 Mae Gwendolyn Henderson, *Speaking in Tongues & Dancing Diaspora* (New York: Oxford University Press, 2014), 62.

45 Brecht, *Brecht on Theatre*, 58.

46 Beyoncé, "Formation," *Lemonade,* Parkwood Entertainment, Musical Recording, 2016.

47 Naila Keleta-Mae, "Get What's Mine: 'Formation' Changes the Way We Listen to Beyonce Forever," *Noisey,* February 8, 2016, https://noisey.vice.com/en_uk/article/beyonce-formation-op-ed-super-bowl-performance-2016

48 Cathy Cohen, "Deviance as Resistance: A New Research Agenda for the Study of Black Politics," *Du Bois Review* Volume 1, Issue 1. (2004): 2.

49 Beyoncé reinforces her role as the wife of Jay-Z in the lyric, "I'm so possessive, so I rock his 'Roc' necklaces." A double entendre, she is referencing both diamonds (rocks) and Jay-Z's management company, Roc Nation. She suggests that by wearing a branded necklace that she exercises her possession over him. Her role as mother is highlighted by the inclusion of her daughter in the video, and through the lyric "I like my baby heir with baby hair and afros."

50 Beyoncé, "Formation," *Lemonade,* Parkwood Entertainment, Musical Recording, 2016

51 Angela McRobbie "Settling Accounts with Subcultures: A Feminist Critique," in *Feminism and Youth Culture,"* Second Edition (London: Routledge, 1991), 39.

52 Beyoncé, "Formation," *Lemonade,* Parkwood Entertainment, Musical Recording, 2016

53 Allison P. Davis, "Why Are White People Trying to Ruin 'Formation'?," *New York Magazine, The Cut,* February 26, 2016, http://nymag.com/thecut/2016/02/why-are-white-people-trying-to-ruin-formation.html.

54 Keleta-Mae, "Get What's Mine"

55 Dr. Zandria Robinson, "We Slay, Pat I," *New South Negress,* February 7, 2016, http://newsouthnegress.com/southernslayings/.

56 Ibid.

57 Richard Dyer, *White: Essays on Race and Culture,* (New York: Routledge, 1997), 3.

58 Brecht, *Brecht on Theatre,* 96.

59 Bertolt Brecht, *Brecht on Theatre,* 23.

60 Ibid., 76.

61 Richard Dyer, *The Matter of Images: Essays on Representation* (London: Routledge, 1993), 3.

Repeater Books

is dedicated to the creation of a new reality. The landscape of twenty-first-century arts and letters is faded and inert, riven by fashionable cynicism, egotistical self-reference and a nostalgia for the recent past. Repeater intends to add its voice to those movements that wish to enter history and assert control over its currents, gathering together scattered and isolated voices with those who have already called for an escape from Capitalist Realism. Our desire is to publish in every sphere and genre, combining vigorous dissent and a pragmatic willingness to succeed where messianic abstraction and quiescent co-option have stalled: abstention is not an option: we are alive and we don't agree.